Voices From A Deep Heart
II

Voices From A Deep Heart
II

Baruti Ambakiseye

Writers Club Press
San Jose New York Lincoln Shanghai

Voices From A Deep Heart II

Writers Club Press
an imprint of iUniverse.com, Inc.

For information address:
iUniverse.com, Inc.
5220 S 16th, Ste. 200
Lincoln, NE 68512
www.iuniverse.com

ISBN: 0-595-20166-0

Printed in the United States of America

CONTENTS

Preface vii

Authors Note ix

Why America is the best country in the world
   and how we can be better. xi

THE ESSENCE OF THE ROOT xiii

   FORWARD by Raymond Alexander xiii

   FORWARD by Lawrence Muhammad xviii

VOICES FROM A DEEP HEART II 1

Epitaph 3

ON GROWING UP BLACK IN HOUSTON 33

Baby Warriors 46

The First Is Not That Which Is Physical 51

A LETTER TO A FRIEND:
   TRYING TO CATCH UP WITH MYSELF 57

The Christalization of Tupac Shakur (A Letter To My Son) 63

MELODIES OF A WRITER 68

BENU AND EDUCATION 143

Reflections: (The More I Learn.) 153

PREFACE

The majority of the contents of this book were written between 1987-1990 but a substantial portion has been updated with *new material*. In addition to a forward from the powerfully profound Minister Lawrence Muhammad, this re-edition includes a *new forward* by my father The Honorable Raymond Alexander and four new essays and a reflection by this author. This reading covers many of the various ideas, questions and beliefs I held during this period of time.

The First Essay "On Growing Up Black in Houston" shows some of the frustration and misunderstanding I had growing up. It was written for the Houston Post essay contest and carries an upbeat ending which may or may not be realistic for all Houstonians.

The essay "A Letter to a Friend" was written to a good friend of mine. It shows the searching and groping that I was going thru at the time on the question of GOD's purpose. My book is not meant to preach a doctrine or principle but to show the creative ideas of the writer. While it does contain educational merit without clarity it cannot be used as the only rule.

These are some of the views, the searchings and the questions that led me on my path and reflections upon them today. Mistakes as well as triumphs are included. These writings should give pause for thought. I would like to thank my friends and family who put up with me and believed in me when many times I didn't believe in myself. Foremost, I thank GOD with whose guidance and love I will continue writing.

AUTHORS NOTE

The words of the forward do not necessarily reflect the opinion of the author. However, I have known Lawrence Muhammad all my conscience life. He is my brother. I thank him very much for his introduction.

The Honorable Raymond Alexander is a lifetime educator and a former member of The Texas State Board of Education.

WHY AMERICA IS THE BEST COUNTRY IN THE WORLD AND HOW WE CAN BE BETTER.

On Tuesday September 11th, The world witnessed possibly the beginning of World War III. These horrific events were bestial, animalistic and not fit for human beings.

Only a deep crevice of hate could have sparked such a despicable act. Why do some people around the world hate America so?

What some people from other countries around the world do not understand about America is the value of our Constitution. The Constitution of the United States is a living, growing document. The strength of America is its melting pot status for all who seek the beacon light of freedom. The perpetrators of this crime did not kill only one race of people or one religious group. The perpetrators of this crime killed Blacks, Whites, Hispanics, Asians and Indians. They killed Christians, Muslims, Jews, Hindus, Buddhist, and people of all faiths. This is why this was a crime against humanity.

The Constitution of this country allows an outlet for those who feel they are wronged in some way to vent their grievances. We live by the principles of Freedom of Speech, Freedom of Religion and a right to earn a living wage. We hold these truths to be self evident that all men are created equal.

As a descendent of slaves in America, I understand the pain of injustice. No people have been oppressed in the world more than African people. Our country has not always lived up to our high ideals but we have a Constitution to guide us. We struggle with our destiny to live by our principles that all men are created equal. We are guided by a living document that we aspire to connect with and in our young history of 225 years we have grown more mature and we still have work to do. Despite any problems America may have this is the greatest country in the world.

These beast that committed this act must be treated as dangerous criminals and taken out of the human fabric. They have ceased to be human beings. We must work with the international community to bring these animals of humanity to justice. But when we go out to bring these criminals to justice we must be guided by our high ideas that all men are create equal and bring justice to the world . We should not worsen the problem by killing innocent people in our desire for justice. If we along with the UN need to put troops in the Middle East to make sure that all parties have a fair opportunity to survive we should do it. We must be the beacon light of freedom for the world.

African people in America have survived through the Middle Passage, through Slavery and through Jim Crow laws and oppression because of the hope that lies within the Constitution of this country and the humanity that was found in enough hearts to make a difference. This is the type of hope that we must bring to the people of the world.

In America we have people of all faiths and religions working together in a quilt of humanity that is not perfect but always provides hope that our hearts will find dignity and peace to exist and grow as human beings where our differences become strengths. This is the America we must take to the world one of justice and hope.

Baruti (9/24/01)

THE ESSENCE OF THE ROOT

FORWARD by Raymond Alexander

Most things in life depend on your perception, How you look at things. Prejudice was a matter of perception. Whites perceived Blacks as not having much sense, not being capable. That's what they were taught and over time they came to believe it. Of course it wasn't true. But they acted on their perception even though it had no bearing on real interpersonal relationships.

In my life time I have seen some great men and studied the lives of many more. Before blacks were allowed to play baseball; whites perceived blacks couldn't play the sport. It was a matter of perception. No one took the time to analyze why for many years until Jackie Robinson. That's just the way it was. Just like it was thought black people couldn't fly a plane until the Tuskeegee Airman proved that theory was incorrect.

It was known in the beginning that I was going to college by everybody in the neighborhood. I didn't have any money but we knew some way I would go to college.

In the 40's we wanted the right to prove ourselves and get better treatment. Kids today have those rights but most don't seem to want to do anything. Some of them don't want to work. In the 40's if someone would have told me that I would work at UH (University of Houston), I would have thought them crazy. We couldn't even walk across the campus. Police would have stopped you before you even stepped foot across it, unless you were a janitor or something. If you had a fine car traveling across the country people wouldn't even you sell you gas unless you dressed up in a chauffeur or maids uniform. You could not go to graduate school in Texas. You had to go out of state. Texas paid the difference in out of state fees for you to go somewhere else. Niemann Marcus would not let you into their store unless your boss called first no matter how much money you had.

Success is a matter of perception. Success is in the eyes of the beholder. I think success is being happy and having enough of the things you need. First of all doing what you feel is right and pleasing to your creator. A lot of people think success is having a lot of money and having a lot of education but success is nothing without pleasing your creator.

And that success begins with taking care of your family. Love of family is the beginning of love of GOD.

I believe all my children have done okay. I wish they were a little more thrifty, but they have done okay. If there was one thing I wish I had taught them better it's how to manage their money. I bear some of the blame for the problems of my children and indirectly my grandchildren have had. I tried to do my best.

Discipline is one of the most important things I wish I had taught. Many people who have talent but don't have discipline don't succeed and many who have a little talent but have discipline succeed. Discipline is developed at a young age from the environment the child has. After a certain age it's hard to have discipline if you haven't been disciplined before. It's hard for a guy that gets to be 40 years old to be disciplined if he hasn't learned that by then. If you haven't taught them something by the time they're seven or eight your going to have a hard time.

When a child reaches the state of mind like those in the Arkansas shootings I'm not sure what should be done. Things you probably should do cannot be done. We have to change their way of thinking. But how do you do that in a democratic society where if you wope or barely talk firmly to them their crying child abuse. I do think the death penalty is a little harsh though at a young age. But things like paddling and the flogging like they do in Singapore are okay. That's why they are ahead of us in education. It seems to have done some good; they don't have the crime we do.

All my children are family oriented and doing okay. They have trouble from time to time but they are doing ok. When they were growing up, I thought Phillip and Ray might be great track men and great scholars. I thought Phillip was going to be an engineer, as a little boy you could see how he tried to take things apart and figure them out. But Ray and Phillip didn't apply themselves like their sister Melanie. Melanie earned a scholarship to TSU (Texas Southern University) when she was going to Worthing High school. She didn't take it because the Jehovah's Witness faith encouraged her not to go. They said she might fall into bad association in college. Later, when she saw how difficult it was, she went to school and did quite well.

I thought Carl would be a great student. He was adequate but he wasn't a great student. If he had liked to go to school like I like to go to school he would have had a lot more accomplishments.

I believe I have been respected because I'm an educator and tried to do something for people, and because I have lived awhile. I guess my family looks at me as having some knowledge of the world.

I tried to live by the golden rule of do onto others as you want others to do onto you. Things some people get upset about I don't get upset about. Sometimes this has come back to haunt me because people do not necessarily live by the same principles I do. Things like TSU firing me because I didn't follow the image they wanted me too. Things like road rage and other things people get upset at I don't get upset at. When you argue with a fool there are two fools arguing.

I wish when I came out of the army I would have bought some property at Prairie View , then I could have got it for a dollar an acre. Or I wish had invested some money in places like IBM and then I wouldn't have to worry about anything. I wish I had bought more land but we were sort of afraid. Most of us in this neighborhood (Hillwood) had lived during the depression so we were a little conservative.

If I won the lottery I would travel then try to do something in education to help. I would return to Italy to see the places I was at during World War II, Rome and Naples. I would go to Jersulaem to see the Holy City and to Damascus the oldest city in the world. I heard a young man say if he won the lottery he would party all the time. This is one of the problems with perception.

Being on the state board was one of my greatest accomplishments. Even when I was kicked off the board by Joe Kelly Butler and the gang I knew I would be back. I tried to be a pioneer for my family to try to start some type of value system of hard work, education and treating your fellowman by the golden rule.

Why is education so important? It teaches a skill that everyone needs. Any society is based on reading, writing and arithmetic. if you can't master basic skills your in trouble. Dexter Manley (A former NFL football star) could play football but he couldn't read so he would get into trouble. The reason is he didn't know what to do with what he had. Public education in America is not working because there is no discipline. Kids don't think education is important. They see all these people making big money who didn't do well in school and say why should I waist my time. We used to learn for the sake of learning. Nobody does that anymore. Kids want to know how its going to help them financially right now. They'll say I can learn more on the street than in school. What they mean is they can make more money on the street right now than in school. But how long will that last?

We should use the Joe Clark approach. Get rid of the bad students to save the good. Everybody can't be saved. European education does not try to teach everybody. At a certain period, they send the children out into the work world if they are not doing well in school.

We are going to have to drastically alter the environment the kids are raised in to change our education system. Parents can't do as much today as they did in my day. What can parents do to the kids? Many students don't see anything wrong with cursing out an old lady. None of the kids in my day gave teachers the problems these kids today do. In my day they wouldn't have done that; if they had tried they would have gotten up off the floor. Drugs are different today also. When I came along there were no drugs out there like they are now. Marijuana was basically the only thing and alcohol had come back from prohibition. Today you can't do as much to discipline kids and they know it. The Administration and the legislature often times look at you as the problem and you would end up in court or something. The whole community must become a part of raising a child. We must go back to the extended family structure; where everyone in the community looks out for the best interest of the child and he could not play one party against another. Every kid tries to play one parent against another. My kids were no different. Teachers against parents, Grandparents against parents, even a little kid learns and uses these tactics.

Carl can make the difference with his young son Jalen, my grandson and my granddaughter Janiya. Both parents are very important in raising a child. They must have consequences for their actions and teach the children to respect what you say. They must be fair and firm and he and his wife must be on the same page.

I would still like to accomplish something on the internet, in stock trading, education or something helpful and help my kids and grandkids. I am glad I had the privelegde in my lifetime of seeing men like Martin Luther King, WEB Dubois, and FDR and learning about men like Booker T. Washington and Abraham Lincoln. There is a statement that best exemplifies my feelings about life by Edwin Markum, *"There is a destiny that makes all men brothers, none goes his way alone all that we send into the lives of others comes right back into our own"*.

Our extended family is very important. It is the root of what we will become. It gives us the foundation to succeed. If all extended families lived by the golden rule, we would have a better world.

FORWARD by Lawrence Muhammad

When I met Carl Louis Alexander in the third grade, he was different than anybody I had ever met before, frail, but not to the point of fear. When I say frail, I mean in stature, body size, weight, poundage and I had come out of Blueridge where I was basically the smallest thing on the street and had to fight just to have fun. And moving and meeting a man named Carl Alexander, someone who had a genuine concern for peace and a light of friendship shined from his eye was a totally different thing for me.

He was not an experimenter: for he was a listener, a listener to his mother. He took her word as stone and he carried that stone with him everywhere he went. I can recall the first experience with cigarettes. And he denying he wanted to try it. We laughed and called him scary. I think were in junior high at the time and just were experiencing cigarettes and stupid smoking at school and we would come home in the evening to share experiences and this was the new thing to see how cool we could be. We didn't know the direction we were heading. All of our lives were affected by pressures greater than ourselves.

I would attribute our success-what we call success today having a job-to a competitive spirit that was instilled in us through little league, through competitions at home, always wanting to run against the other, whether it was a bicycle race, whether it was sticks in the mud, whether it was boxing, weather it was wrestling, whether it was lifting weights, always wanting to be a winner in that circle. So as we started to face life, as you saw friend number 1 get to peg one, friend number two get to peg two, you just knew that you were going to get to peg one or two sooner or later because you've always's been in that race and you knew you couldn't lose because that race was right in your way of doing things. You said if they can do it I'm gonna be right on their tails and eventually I'm gonna pass em up. This was our attitude. This is what kept us moving in the right direction.

I succumbed to some peer pressures growing up but within myself and the upbringing I received I had a scale of balance. So that when I experienced things that the peer pressures had I had a better chance to weigh them. Love was on one side of the scale and the situation was on the other side of the scale. It gave me the opportunity to weigh the circumstances and beliefs of what my life should be. This way love and family life, outweighed some of the pressures of drugs and outweighed some of the pressures of bad conduct. I didn't have to succumb to one and make a choice. I was able to deal within the pressures and balance it out and then make a choice. I thank my parents. My parents made me who I am today. They molded me not from the time of my birth up until my 29 years of living but in the womb my mother shaped me in her mind of the kind of man she wanted me to be, not knowing, in reality, that I would be the man I am at this moment. And she doesn't know me fully at this moment. For the world shaped me too. And now I am reshaping myself into the formation that my mother and father wanted me to be in from that seed, that ovary, the egg shape and mental thought. I'd like to say thank you to them for giving me the opportunity to fail and when I failed I was not pushed down but I was lifted up. I was looking for the fancy things of life. I couldn't conceive at the time that what I needed was around me all the time. Love, good home, friendships is heaven in all walks of life. They provided me with heaven and I didn't even know it. None of us knew we had heaven.

Carl saw his father as different with no definition just different. Growing up, certain comments, he doesn't wope me, he doesn't use file language, he listens to opera, he always has a comment or two about things, people easily use him, I'm confused about this person, yeah or nay, not good or bad just different. As time went on rebellion against the difference. Still not understanding the difference but looking at the differences being wrong instead of right. Saying "Had he been this way, I would have done this. Had he been that way I could have improved myself by doing this. Had he improved himself to the vision that I think he should have been in then I would have been much further along than I would have been". Blaming all his interior faults on a person who did not effect him in those negative ways. But he had to find some place to put his faults because no one wants to accept all their own burdens.

Around this time, my friend Carl had a sister to come to birth. A confusing birth to him as I watched as he sought to understand how his space was now being invaded. A new experience for him, unexpected. My brother Carl's sister was born with a birth deficiency which added to the pressures on my brother. Knowing his emotional feelings for responsibility I believe he began to take this on as his total responsibility. And then the pressures came. Pressures for acceptance, pressures for rebellion. See,we all rebel, it is just a matter of why to determine whether we rebel in good conscience or not. He began to rebel against that stone that he once carried around and threw it down. He started to drink, he started to smoke, he started to have fun, societal fun, to alleviate some of the realities that needed to be addressed. As we got closer to graduation and things were looking a little better, Carl was not able to recognize what he was up against and he was not able to recognize his inner beauty. He began to place the external beauties of life as the only true beauties of the world. And he began to live other than self. So we managed to stumble by a few nights of intoxication, a moment of love, a moment of fighting, a moment of rebellion and we managed to make it to a place called Prairie View A&M University. This is when you get a better chance to see someone for who they really are when you live with them. You could see Carl had lived a sheltered life. His chores were at a menial level. At home he didn't have to do as many things as he had to try to do now. Ironing and making his bed and preparing himself for the day, it was a new experience but at the same time it was an escape from reality away from home , able to deal with the new pressures now. And there was a new pressure out there, it was called she. How many she's can you have? Again not able to recognize our own inner beauty at our own pace causing more pressure on ourselves. So my brother began to work on himself, taking on all these things, and they were mounting on one side but there was another man on the other side fighting. This fellow has all these things on his heart and mind. Internally he wasn't fighting at first but now he began to fight back. I'll cut back on this or I'll break away from this or I'll show my independence by doing this or I'll stand up to them all. He began to be a very rebellious person. I mean every time you say hi, its like what cha say hi for, I'll kick your ass. Showing his strength externally instead of internally. The internal beauty that I had seen in him at age 8 was almost gone. It was almost all gone. But then he finally began to try to reach to his inner beauty, recognizing his inner beauty as the most precious gift. After he graduated from Texas Southern, he began to make moves on what he wanted to do. Sometimes falling, sometimes going in the dark where there ain't been no light but still striving. Striving to the expectations of self. Striving to expectations of GOD. He still has rebellion to those who love him, and I guess he always will but on a scale of 1 to 10, he's an 11.

There's a word that explains our lives as we grew up and that word is family. I don't think we looked at each other in any other manner than family. I can recall the third grade, the walk to school was even set up in a manner that we could look after one another because it was in a cycle. First one would pick the second one up, second would then get the third, third would get the fourth and fourth would get the fifth and wait there, and almost do it like clockwise. You could tell by the clock if somebody wasn't going that day and turn backwards on the mornings when it was extremely cold and walk backward because the wind would whip your face. After school, though we were in different classrooms we met at the bridge to walk together not for a safety factor but just to see a friend, the family back in tack again. It was like a shell around the egg, it was a peel like around the orange, around that family to walk home again. As we grew and left that era and left and went off to middle school, we rejoiced again at the bridge to see the family return and walk home again. The bus would come and even though they didn't come at the same time we would wait 5,10,15,20 minutes, whatever for the friend to return. We went on to high school and got cars and all worked and picked each other up from work to see if the family was okay. This was our family, this was our life.

Our life growing up was different than the youth of today. The youth today has no example. He has no immediate example to follow. If he tries to follow the life of his parents, his parents are living in the high statistical rate of 60 to 70% divorce. If he tries to follow the example of brothers and sisters then he's looking at fornication or he's looking at many transgressions against the supreme being that we know of or I believe in and he has no example. He must look within himself to find to find root knowledge of who he is, what he should be, what he can be. He cannot go on the expectations of the world or the educational system. He has to go from his internal belief, that genesis, or that genetic code within himself that will teach him the root of his loin. He must trace his bloodline. He should look back into his historical bloodline to see if he's a king or a prince. He should remain in that bloodline by not taking on his circle but looking at his historical root to find out where he should be.

Education for me did not provide the foundation I needed. I never received the definition of why and I was a man of many questions and little questions like why had to be answered or I didn't have the perfect paper in my mind. My parents told what was good but didn't tell me why. Education is good to have to be able to succeed in society but I did not put forth effort to receive education even though I have a Masters degree and 3/4ths of an E.E. D. I probably have run the race at 1/3rd my capability. I know my mind is much stronger but it turned into a game. Education did not give me the foundation I needed.

I hear the term miseducation so often I prefer to say loop hole education. Someone took from the book of education out of it the things they want to teach and created a curriculum. Whereas there's a bigger book that they say they don't have time to get to all of that. Your not miseducated, you're educated but you got to have a will to go to the major book, if you want the entire circle of education, meaning travel, meaning world knowledge. In my home I'm going to take out a part because I can't teach it all but if you want it all you've got to go to that world book. The world book is the quest for world knowledge. History of not only Texas, history not only of the U.S. but history of Africa, history of the British nation, history of Germany, history of all the greats that have come before us. When you get a feeling for education it's like dope. It's like reading, once you love to read it's like dope, you just can't put it down. When you get a quest for education it's like dope. You're on a mental high when you learn something new, GOD. It just freaks you out to read something and find something new. I think that is where the miseducation comes in because when you're educating multiethnic groups then you have to hit those things in their life that make them say GOD! I didn't know this, instead of saying same old thing all over again and never seeing yourself, that is the purpose of education but I don't think a miseducation was purposely done.

If we had had a complete education we would have known what racism was. Racism is something that is seen by people who are looking for it. And until I actually looked for it, I never saw it. My mind was preoccupied with the things that made my world go round and I wasn't concerned with racism growing up. Even though I went to James H. Law Elementary and maybe had six white students in the whole building we knew nothing of this. Even though I went to Dick Dowling Middle School where we became a minority and had the M to M transfers we knew nothing of this. We just knew that we were in the school some blacks hung together, some whites. Even though I went on to Jones High School with maybe five whites in the whole building, we still knew nothing of this. Because it wasn't looked for, we weren't global.

Growing up as a child you had few experiences in education. An education, is designed to keep you out of the frays of understanding racism. If we had been under the understanding of what South Africa was then we would have known racism did exist. This was not taught. I would have to say I had no encounters with racism growing up because I was not looking for it. However, your education affects your mind set, your thinking. I had no inferiority to the next person as far as stature but in general yes. For I was considered a poor reader, a poor speller and a poor writer. I was considered by the educational system as retarded I'd almost say because I was in special education courses. So I definitely was on one of the most likely not to succeed list. But that internal thing, nobody actually knows who you really are. I took on those characteristics because once you give a person a report of himself every six weeks for a great deal of his life, he begins to believe that that report card he saw, 3 "F's" and an "A"; only in P.E. I made an "A". I began to believe that the only thing I could do was play. So it put in me a desire not to go any further in this because I had failed at it so often. But my family kept me going. I have to say to the author of this book who used to tell me the letters from afar in the classroom so that I could spell America and pass the spanking of the day, those kind of things are very meaningful today.

This man, Carl Alexander is one of the smartest men I have ever known. When he tells me something I know he speaks with knowledge. Also, because I know him deeply, I know his faults. He is a man of love but not weak love. He believes in the power of love. He believes in its commitment. He believes in developing that love far beyond expectations and imaginations. His relationships with women can be summed up in one humorous word. Fear. He is cautious about sharing his heart because that is the source of his life. His strongest points are his flexibility, being able to adapt to the situation as needed and to go the extra step. He has a controlled aggression and focus when he sets his sights on a goal but only when he sets his sights. His weaknesses and mistakes come when he has a lack of knowledge or when he gets down on himself. He sees easy solutions but sees no one coming with these simple solutions and it becomes frustrating. When you can see things but don't have the power to change things then you become frustrated. When you see things that should be affected, could be affected and you believe is going to be affected, yet time drags on, it's nonacceptance. You have a difference with the system. This is the Carl Alexander I know.

Today there is a little better understanding between Carl and his father. After looking back and forward, being 29 and able to remember when dad was close to 29, what he had to be experiencing and how life had to be even more difficult for him in his time as a black man, there is a little better understanding. Now knowing that he is facing some of the same things that dad faced and maybe not doing as well as he did at the time when he was that age. So maybe those differences were all right, he just didn't realize what it was. Now coming to understand he had discipline, now understanding and seeing him as a greater person than we ever saw him because we understand now. We all fall short to some of the sinful things of life, it's just whose devil are you battling and whose devil am I battling because we all have our battles. Today there is a much better understanding of who a person is and what they've gone through.

Carl and I have some disagreements, there are some differences. However, we both understand the plight of the black man today. We understand that we must live differently other than our fathers or our grandfathers because we have to give our youth an example. We're in total agreement today that money is not the most sought after thing for happiness in life but it is something we seek to have.

We're both in agreement that understanding your brother and forgiving your brother is better than killing and shooting and stabbing your brother. We're in total agreement today that when you have a family, you should try to maintain that family and should not play games with the word marriage. You should try to do the best you can. We're in total agreement on all those things. Religiously, I am a Muslim; he is not. He chooses to examine all religions, looking for the one that meets his spiritual needs. But Carl and I agree that religion is not in a book, it's not in the Bible or the Holy Koran. It's in the genetic makeup of a man. Righteousness. If I can believe in being a righteous man. I had never read in a book anywhere in my life before I knew that certain things were not correct. Stealing, no one really put up on aboard that you shouldn't break into a man's home and hit his wife upside the head and take his vacuum cleaner, you just shouldn't do that, that's in the genetic makeup of a man. To tell a lie, even when you're a young child, it disturbs your insides to lie, it's just in the genetic makeup of a man.

This is the type of man Carl Louis Alexander is. His true potential is yet to come. The struggle is just beginning.

VOICES FROM A DEEP HEART II

Epitaph

Ralph Waldo Emerson

There is a time in every man's education when he arrives at the conviction that envy is ignorance; that imitation is suicide; that he must himself for better or for worse as his portion; that though the wide universe is full of good no kernel of nourishing corn can come to him but through his toil bestowed on that plot of ground which is given him to till. The power that resides with him is new in nature, and none but he knows what that is which he can do, nor does he know until he has tried.

From "Self Reliance"

THE WIND AGAINST THE SPIRIT

The mighty wind bellows its force against the staggering spirit inside.
The wind sends me fearful and cringing back and forth from the sanctity
   of my dwelling.
I stand against its force, alone, naked, powered only by spirit's divine faith.
From its midst, the wind echoes laughter and contempt at my plight.
Harks of wretchedness are hurled in my direction.
I hear the wind whistles its epithets, too little, too dumb, too dark, too
   wild, too filled with fright.
Forever it wishes to block my path; at every turn, every corner, every open-
   ing, it's there to halt, to block, to stop my every glimmering bright.

It is cold and unrelenting, never letting up for a moment for fear I might
   break its current if it gives any light.
Filled with the dutiful masses, the wind seeks you to ride.

It wishes you to come soullessly; it wants you to accept its protected com-
   forts and refuse to make a fight.

It wants you to give in smiling even though you feel it just isn't right.

Against thou, I the spirit must make my stand.

I used to want to sail the wind but now I refuse to ride.
The spirit holds the greater, more truthful power that lets me battle this
   wretched tide.

With the Lord as my teacher and leader, I must always fight the wind.
With my last drop of blood, my spirit will clash thee to the end.

SO EMPTY AND YET SO FULL

Being living being on this earth, we are filled with wondrous hope and life, free to enjoy the fruits of nature.
Yet there is an emotion which if left unexplored or unexposed will soon make the spirit empty.

This emotion is the most powerful resource known to man. It can push man to the brink of obsession or to limits previously thought not inside of thee.

When someone finds that spark, that emotion, that stimuli, nothing in this world can keep them from trying to achieve it.

With it there's a feeling of indestructible passion, a conqueror of all obstacles.
Without it there's an entity empty, longing to touch the fire and feel it burning inside of them.

Everyone is looking for this place, this kind of pot of gold, this instance when the meaning becomes clear and when the question is answered.
Something or someone who's very presence inspires good, the best and sustains it.
Everyone assumes the stars are always bright and the sun always shines for those who are smiling.

But without the filling of this yearning the world is dark even though my eyes see.
The things we have are never enough because we always want more.

We have everything but we also have nothing.
We are living beings but yet we are not alive.
We are millionaires but yet we are still poor.

We are following a course of action but still our mission is undefined.
We are naive but yet experience makes us so worldly.

Our lives are empty but as long as we are living we are full.

For me destiny awaits or maybe that's an oblivious dream.

But I tell you, you hold the key to my power to make my blind eyes see a
world unseen.

CLA (87)

FREEDOM LET NOT BE WASTED

Freedom let not be wasted, let's carry on the never ending fight. Harder and harder let's try to appreciate the freedom our forefathers fought so hard to attain.

Be zealous, aspiring, striving and ambitious in your struggle and let nothing keep you from the top.

May the blood of great men cry as we bask in the sun.
Should not we be struggling for more rights instead of rights of struggles already done?

Tested and tempered, no one else wants to be our friend so we might as well be our own.

Why do we blame our plight on the color of our skin when its the quality of our character that is being put to the test?

We need to get strength from ourselves, trust in GOD and not worry about the rest.

The will to succeed comes from the mind; so let not color be your stumble, because the only power in the eyes of power is monetarily defined.
So let us stop fighting and killing one another and let not complacency reach our soul, maybe then freedom will not be wasted and a man named Martin will have achieved his goal.

CLA (82)

THE TRAP

I'm trapped in a trap with a steel curtain grip.
Its claws cling deep into my soul.
From my pouring blood it squeezes and pounces every breathing drip.
Its terror is the coldness by which this terror grows.
The burning terror has a name, one which I care not to repeat.
Every time I hear her voice it's a painful melody.
I've asked it to make up its mind, does it wish me killed or will it wait on
    destiny.
No matter what I say or do though, this terror won't release.

I've begged, pleaded, tried to reason but still it insists on bludgeoning.
It has no heart, a face unmoved, an emotion that for me, maybe only me
    has no feeling.
Yet at times I feel a light, a tiny crack, that lets me think my fate is not at
    its ending.
But just as soon as hope lifts me up, twirling into the depth it's sending.

What did I do to deserve this hurt?
What's the evil spell that cast this dungeon?
What sin of mine led to this fate?
Is this his divine curse for my sin of an insurmountable something?

The glowing casket shines so pretty but inside lurks like a venomous cat.
Devouring and demeaning all that dare enter her realm. Unbeknownst
    come in flocks but may never find their way back.

Does it truly know the severity of the pain it inflicts. Slowly wringing dry
   all my heart felt passion?
Why couldn't it have killed me all once at once?
If it had told of impending death, I would have readied my mind for that
   action.
But it has led me a cauldron of circles.
Up and down, in and out, will this yo-yo ever flinch. I think like hell I
   could unshackle its back
But first its closeness must be lynched.

Caught in this trap I have missed so much
The world outside is beautiful and full of life out there. But instead I am
   caught in this clinging trap. I can only look at this heartless wall and
   stare.

If I should survive, never again will this trap catch me near.
Oh, I may play with its borders a lot.
But never will it curse my blood again,
I won't be caught in its devious plot.

The daggers it throws hurt too much.
It splinters my skin no matter where I lead my shay. But one day soon
   someone will break the jail of this encasing nut.
I can't wait to see the awakening of the day, of the dee.

(CLA) 88

JUST A LITTLE OF YOUR SUNSHINE COULD CHANGE THE WORLD

Just a little of your sunshine could change the world.
Your magnetism the sweetest, the aura of an angel and beauty beyond compare.
GOD must have placed you here on this earth to show us a little bit of what heavens like.
For Every time I see you, I cannot imagine a more heavenly sight.

If you only knew your power, how you could touch so many lives. How with your smile, you could silence a room, of angry shouting men. How with your touch, you could ease the hurt of a lifetime of many painful wounds.
How your voice echoes of enchantment, strengthened you could speak to a hundred needy ears.
Cause what you have is sunshine girl, and just a little could help change the world.
Like Helen of Troy before you, many men would fight for your hand.
They would lock you in a castle out of reach from all the world.
But your destiny is sharing your love with people, Cause just a little of your sunshine, just a little, could help change my world.

Your every beautiful flower and every sweet fragrance known to man.
Your every gentle thought and every kind word ever heard. Even when your heart turns cruel, behind your dark exterior a ray of sunshine always breaks through.

Your every fantasy and every destiny, cause what you have is sunshine and
just a little could help change the world.

Right now your glow is hidden, in a shroud filled with silence.
But soon your shine will glare like the brightness of the sun.
It can't be bottled up forever; he would not allow such cruelness.
Another chance at heaven may never come along.

Please don't fear those who love you; they will cater to your noble whims.
Don't chase them away because they wish to be near you; let your love
guide their steps.
Welcome and cherish their attention, because just a little of your sunshine
may help change their world.

Don't be selfish, don't be impatient, find the strength to love and not just
those whom you like, because your love can help many people, let lives
be your cause;
just a little of your sunshine could help make everything right.

Those of us walking in the rain need you.
Give us your umbrella of sunshine to help clear our path.
Never let your smile leave us. Never let your sweet voice become coated,
let us forever hear your laugh.
Instill us with your friendly spirit, that let's us know hope is always in our
grasp.

Shenee, I know your true worth, don't let yourself be locked in.
Grow in vibrancy, vitality, honesty, courage and strength.
And know you have what the world needs more of.
Cause with just a little of your sunshine, so much love you could bring.

CLA (88)

TO BE IN LOVE

When you're in love, you run the gambit of emotion.
Through every little step, you feel your heart cutting open.
It is a feeling that can cut like a lengthened, jagged knife.
When you care for someone with all your life.

Love is really such a mysterious, funny thing.
It can give you so much joy and so much pain.
To be in love is a state of dream like reality.
You are running across the clouds and looking down on the rainy sunshine
running free.

Love is the extreme of every emotion and every fantasy.
It is like a two edge sword, one side cuts the other side bleeds.
Your joyous occasion is not matched by any other exhilaration or high
filled in the most gregarious celebration.
But its pain is so debt filled and stabbing like and endless flight down a
treacherous, perilous waterfall sensation.

When you smile, the blooming flowers swell you up in a basking, flow-
ing web.
When you frown, cancer drips a dying tear to an indestructible rock bed.

Nothing else can be so up and down, so extreme, so passive, so sweet, so
real.
It can pull you and push you until it takes away all your sane will.

To be in love cannot be compared to the goldest gold or the richest riches.
It has a glory all its own, creating and conquering all odds and following
its own course and mission.

When you truly love someone there is nothing else that really can compare.
There is nothing else that you can think of. All the money, image and
prestige cannot compare,
Because the greatest feeling in the world is to be in love.

CLA (88)

FEAR NOT FIGHT ON

Yes, I fear the darkness. It stands before me like a concrete wall.
Should I creep into its shadows further?
Do I dare venture where I might fall?
Do I stand still in its terror or do I look deep into its midst?
If I do not go, will I know if the fear were really a fear to fear?

Even though they say I can't will I have the courage to say I can?
If I test their power will it hold?
Will I attack the darkness or will I remain afraid?
For a Sigma man there is really only one way.
Our obstacles are great but we will always stand tall.

Be it courting the most beautiful lady, or holding our family strong or
    fighting our civil battles till death, ye mighty host will march on.
With GOD as my power and glory there is nothing to fear today,
Fear not fight! That is the Phi Beta Sigma way.

Spring 1983
Delta Theta
Prairie View A&M
University

I AM ME

I am somebody because I'm special and there's no one else like me.
I respect me, love me, can't get along without me, so I try to be the best me
   I can be.

I am intelligent and likeable, naive and worldly. I am ambitious, loving,
   caring and no one knows this better than me.
That is why I am the best there is to me.

CLA (85)

PRETTY KIDS

Imagine for a second if we couldn't see with our eyes but only with our
heart and mind.
Our voices would then be only a transport of ideas of our sensitive
thoughts inside.
Minus we'd be of the sensation of beauty, but minus also I guess to the
visual breath take of beauty.

Pictures need not impair judgement and color our perception of what we
can be.
But I ask who in the world said your pretty?

Can you describe the color red to someone so blind? Can you make them
understand its hue and rhyme?
A child's mind might be like the color red. Only knowing the allusion and
reality of things they see and hear that soon fill their head.
Can we really tell what someone will one day be, when we say they're the
ones that are so pretty?

Just what is this pretty state of mind?
Is it a miracle given from up above to those who deep down are just flesh
and blood?
Just who was it that said that you're so pretty and fine?

Are you pretty because of what you say or do or is their something in your
eyes too?

If it's really true that we're all the same then were we meant at all to carry away in this pretty game?

We see everybody is dark and everybody is light. Everybody has things to hate and things to like. Everyone is ugly but everyone too can be so pretty and be whatever they want to be.
Pretty lies within our innermost soul. It can lay forever but with love we will see it's power and value grow and grow.

But we now still think that that is which appears to be. (1)
Illusion and image dominate our reality.
But who in the world said that I'm so pretty?
The world is me and pretty is for everyone in it to see.

CLA (87)

(1) Thoreau-"Where I lived and what I lived for".

THE BATTLE OF THE CHILDREN

If I could shelter a life away from pain would that life be my own?
Worthy I am, but my bitterness is already shown.
It would seem but a waste.
My mental notebook is still filled with hardened memories that could
never ever be erased.
Mine would be a biased perfection.

But what about the children or what about the childlike heart?
Those who have not as yet seen the pain start. What if we could shelter
them? What if we could shield them from pain?
Do they really have to learn to cry, to learn?
Should they have to struggle, starve and sin to survive because their heart
yearns?

If we traded places would we really fair any better?
Would we not still feel the pain of unwantedness, the sting of indifference
and the loneliness of the unloved?

Would we also begin to cry out and curse the world and feel no loyalty to
those above?
Yet the children must continue their battle.

They must battle the man who tries to give them powder and say it's sugar.
They must battle those who try to defile them because they are little.
They must battle a picture that tries to tell them what they should and
should not believe.

And must battle a world really hard sometimes to conceive.
They have not all the battles won but yet and still they must battle on.

Is it really true we only become strong by experiencing pain?
But a sheltered heart would not have to play that game.
They would only know honesty, joy and love and live a life we could only
dream of.
But the power of shelter is not now in our grasp.
Just our continuing fight to help our children get past.

CLA (87)

THE UNCOMFORTABLE

What fears you today you beautiful one?
Is the danger real, hot and fire breathing?
Will is scratch our your eyes if you look at it?
Can it destroy your mind and soul if you try to talk to it?

Is the answer to run away and hide, never to face the darkness? Can we
camouflage ourselves in a dark closet hoping the fear goes away?
Should we hide in the latrine and hope our Uncomfortable doesn't wish to
wait today?

Easier it is to turn away, to run, to walk another path or another road to
get away from the feeling. But can we ever get away from the
Uncomfortable? It will follow you like a shadow, carrying your with it.

Is it really better to try? Won't tomorrow bring a new fear? If we face our
fears, maybe we could find a new balance, a new secret, maybe a new
part of yourself that we never knew existed.

"Fear always springs from ignorance. It is a shame if your tranquility, amid
dangerous times arises from the presumption that like sheltered women
and children yours is a protected class and that you can seek a tempo-
rary peace by diverting your thoughts away from tough questions or
issues or not dealing with those different from you, hiding your head
like an ostrich in the flowering bushes. Look closely is the danger still a
danger, is the fear any worse. Turn and face the uncomfortable, look

deep into its eye and search its nature, and inspect its origin. If you can stand against it and look it in the eye, you will pass on superior."*

The world belongs to those who test the unknown, not those who are only comfortable with what they know or like. If you gain something you know what is the mystery? What do you have to do?
But if you encounter something unknown and stand and meet it's challenge, you will be of more value with your new knowledge.
The shapers turn something that is uncomfortable or something they don't like into something that is very comfortable, something that is now very well liked.

If you are not a shaper then you will be shaped. You will end up being a mold in that comfortable likeness, to run like they run and laugh like they laugh, you will lose what is unique about you.

Fear, anxiety and uncomfortable are human traits of the uninformed and unknowing.
But those who open their eyes and meet that challenge will never have to ask which way they should be going. And those who care not to know or try, will only be part of a limited class.
But outside of their teachers reign they will be lost like the largeness of a donkeys ass.
If you do not wish to search, to ask and face the challenge never, chances are that whatever you do, whomever you meet, you'll remain uncomfortable forever.

CLA (88)
*Ralph W. Emerson (American Scholar)

ECSTASY AND THE DARK PEARL

She washed up onto the shores of my destiny.
The world really knew not this heaven but she is heaven just the same.
Her innocence is protected by a vague, sharp edge.
Her passion is buried deep inside her shell.

Her shine blinds me and binds me whenever she's in my reach.
She is my opposite, for I am rough and have followed a darkened path.
But in her sight she gives me light,
Just a little of her shine illuminates my cast.

She is not fragile, I know for I've pressed her corners.
She is strong and fights back with a coldness that could cool the flames of
    hell.
When she feels pressure, she will shine her light no more, she will not
    weave her magical spell.

Though not grasping for attention, she stands out in the crowd. Among
    all the beautiful pearls of the world, she shines the brightness, she is the
    dark pearl.
Her darkness adds to her elegance, a shadowy glow, a mysterious heavenly
    complexion. She is the darkest pearl, a pure vision of ecstasy.

She arouses and stimulates every emotion, inflames every low burning fire.
    Her aroma, her aura, her essence, spellbound the most tested of ship
    weary travelers.
She is my willing trap; cast my anchor into her sea.

Let me drown into her depths and be lost in her waters forever still.

Like the sirens of Ulysses, it's impossible to resist her captive singing
    temptation.
So untie my shackles, let me wind my sail against her treacherous rocks.
Let me guide my compass of passion in her direction.
Hold back that emotion for there is agony in that thought.

I imagine my culmination, me and the dark pearl.
Living under the sea forever with ecstasy being our reward.
The color of our water is red and our well will never run dry.
Together we will make a shade darker, a new little pearl, who will teach the
    world to shine.
Our strength will come from nature, it will invigorate our hearts.
The birds will sing, and the kids will play because our dark sunshine will
    fill the earth.
Darkness is from where we came, sunshine is to where we'll go.
Darkness reminds of our beginning, shine tells of new glows.

Once you were a used, ugly duckling, today you dark pearl stand tall.
But there are other ducklings out there you could bring with you, I won't
    rest till I shine with them all.

Ecstasy and the dark pearl have a oneness in their soul.
Ecstasy is my passion and the dark pearl my goal.
To cultivate and caress her fluids will appease my driving surge.
But to satisfy my passion, ecstasy and the dark pearl must be in oneness
    for the world.

CLA (88)

ON ANTICIPATION OF SEX

The urges hit you like a hurricane, powerfully encasing all your being.
At mercy, uncontrollable urges leading you into another world.
Dreams of anticipation, of inward and outward thrust, of up and down
   movement, of flesh wit flesh ecstasy.

Urges feeling you deep inside, with both eyes closed, touching the param-
   eters of another heart.
Your body is about to burst, raging with fiery excitement, the touch, the
   breath, the feel and the passion of love is soaring in your veins.
It carries you away in a euphoric haze, Your thoughts become blurred, to
   morrows run together, only memories of now exist.

Your arms open wide to the call of passion, to be swept away in lust.
Imagination guides your eyes pass the garments of your destiny.
Anticipation of your release entices your urges.
From the first caress your heartbeat quickens.
Engaged, close, the moment of awakening nears.
Your clothes burn on you like a blaze, you relieve them. The essence of life
   is revealed.

The sight of angels, two beautiful bodies bare, nude, natural, ready to
   embrace, to intertwine.
The odor of love enters the air.
The touch is electric, flaming your fire pulling loves liquid to the top.
Your machine becomes erect, all parts functioning, stimulating and
   inviting.

There's no turning back.
You are caught in the grip of a large rolling bolder. Helpless.

Reality dips you beyond conscience boundaries.
Your engrossed totally in the pores of your being. Inside fleshly lubrica-
   tion spurs your adrenaline. Deep you enter, then pull back, deeper
   again then out.
Infinite, repeating pleasure, Your whole body riveting.

Your buttocks tighten, your breast are full, your insides are on fire.
Your tool of trade brings your machine to ultimate culmination.
Ahhhhh…. There's no greater, more powerful feeling in the world.
As the blood rushes back to your head, you can only dream of next time.

THE DAY

Coming, coming, soon the day is coming that we all dread but that we want to see.

We want to see if it will fulfill the prophecies, who will live, who will die. Is there any difference?

Coming, coming, soon the day will come when we'll wonder whether we have been good or bad and whether it really makes any difference.

Soon the day will come when our futility might become evident , when we might appear like ants in water.

Soon the day is coming when evil will have the power no more. Soon the light will shine and drown all the darkness.

Not when but soon the day is coming, when higher love may fill us with joy.

Coming, coming, soon the day is coming when our father will lead us to a brighter day.

Coming, coming, yes, soon the day is coming.

I WONDER

I had a crush on her from the first time I saw her. Her fragrance smelled of
    fresh air.
Her dignity and beauty holds my heart.
When she smiles it covers a glow everywhere.

My she's really wonderful.
I wonder does she know how I really feel? Does she really care?
Does she really know how I care about her and hope her days are filled
    with every lovely cheer?

I feel a spark Every time I pass her room. Exuberance so exquisite like
    flowers in full bloom.
I care for her and hope she is always fine. She has a beauty and loving
    spirit that will never change with the passing of time.

But does she know how I really feel; Does she know who I am?
Does she think I have some ulterior motive or some devious plan?

My, what misconstrued thoughts come to your mind when you don't
    know what's on another persons mind.

Does she really hear my words? Does she really not believe?
I hope she knows that for her I would move ocean and earth, Please with
    my heart don't deceive.
Wonder what she is thinking now.
I wonder how she feels.
I think she may be thinking of me but I guess I'll wonder still.

THE NEW FLOWER

A new flower proved to be in the midst of the tall trees.
She looked out of place or maybe the element was out of she.
The trees had been there longer and told her she didn't belong.
She looked bewildered but started to wonder what makes me so wrong?

Yes you're older and more profound. Yes, you pretty much run the town.
I'm a pretty flower too, now can't you see, I can be a tall flower just as good
     as thee. And isn't it true or maybe it's just me, didn't you start out some-
     thing or just like me.
I can stand tall just you wait and see, one day I'll stand strong just like you
     tree.
I don't have to take your pampering and counsel long, with my own
     branches I will work hard and go on.
I will learn from you tall trees, yes, I will learn it all.

I am at the age of nourish like the bright red sun. My life has really just
     begun.

The new flower looked bewildered and out of place; It was very young
     with no hardened taste.
But now, it became very clear to see that the trees were really envious of
     she.

As the sun shines on her brighter, as the birds drop love unto her breast. In
     this aura, she will grow stronger and be a new tall tree to fill the earth.

CLA (90)

DAGGERS OF GOD

Thee, be but a question to me.
Thee, who knew us before thine eyes could see.
OH yes, faith rations him be true O'er how else did thy become new.

What was his place before thy noble world?
Of his history what has hath?
Or does history have a Babel birth and infinite existence be all his grand.

Pains come onto him, what may they be?
Thy children and creatures be his toil.
Blessed, then cursed, then blessed into sin.
My though his weaklings might sure fall.

Does worry or doubt ever enter his sphere?
Could pride be his for our ketonic state?
Alas, he gives power of will,
But what of a babes for a parents mistake?

Him never tired, never hungry, never distracted from true.
With our sinful minds we know of nothing else to do.
Exalted high atop his governing throne, Did the judger have a judge with
  whom to atone?

Aligned in adverse battle with the lecherous one, to heave, to ho, in tug
  roe thrust over the earthly race.

With chessboard mentality they pull strings in a sandbox puzzle, moving
pieces like pawns to their own dogmatic, immortal taste.

Against this scenic thoust mere mortals must endure, Expected to hold
and walk a noble plan.
Almighty shields his children from his almighty creation.
But the daggers still wound because they are splinters from the daggers of
GOD.

Oh wretched mental majesty thou which has been endowed,
Cursed be the logic with which we can decipher our plight.
Praised be the dumb who are hindered not by intellectual strife.
Unencumbered by questioning analyst they lead a simple life.
But exception be dammed for forever we are pressed to wonder.
What spirit guides our journey thru this perilous path.

The light of his reality carries a painful toil.
Continually the darkness of escape begs to hear our call.
The pointy ear adultery waits wit fiery claws to lead our way.
Her smile is infectious, driving the pangs of evil pleasures deep into our
midst.
At every turn temptation hurtles a jagged dagger against our resolve.

Our vast warrior shines his sincere light low, his rousing voice is drowning
in the sea of overshadowment.
Troubled be his earthly servants mired in this confusion that he beset.
Of equal weight is the cast of good and bad.
Nigh thus wickedness is a golden tempter.

Exposed mightily before our naiveness, its spectacle clearly and attractively
in our sight.
Behold thy servant bound and shackled against this peril.

Weary eyes view his ever redundant calamities, piercing and filling minds with incandescent evil.

The voice of our master is mute but boldly and vividly imprinted for the searchers and receivers. But the messengers of the dragon have a loud intercom of deceit.

Confusion abounds in the minds of the mortal multitudes.
Teetering on the brink of pronounced chaos, they tilt weightlessly on the side of the two vast foes.

Phophesizers of faith sprout of all the answers of love but inside seethe with the very incarnate of hate.
They drench the market of naivete with righteous indignation, with pulsating oratory they catch the masses in an infectious beat.

ON GROWING UP BLACK IN HOUSTON

Everyday after school for two weeks, we ran straight home. First one to Craig's house would get an imaginative gold medal from an imaginative Olympics we participated in. These Olympics and other activities would sometimes get us in trouble. I was supposed to come straight home from school but one day after playing football and staying too long, I got home and my mother was waiting for me. "Didn't I tell you to come straight home from school"? She said holding something behind her back as I entered the house. My first thought was to run, but I knew that when I finally got caught I'd get it worse. My mother's eyes were large with fury as she pulled the belt from behind her and started lashing me.

"Some-times-it-just-seems-like-you-want-to disobey-me", she said lashing at me with every syllable. After she was through she told me to go to my room and wait for my father to come home. I thought to myself, whoever heard of getting a whipping in the sixth grade. I knew my mother would not try to hurt me. She used to say that it hurt her more than it did me to give me a whooping, but I don't remember seeing her crying. I didn't worry about getting whooped again when my father got home. My father hadn't whooped me a day in my life but sometimes I'd rather get a whooping than the speeches he sometimes gave me. He thought of himself as a philosopher. He had numerous degrees and tried to use psychology but seemed not to have any common sense to me. He would sometimes argue a long drawn out time about the same thing and accomplish no change. I wanted him to take an active interest and show me some attention sometime. But he never seemed to be around to me.

Growing up in Houston during the late 60's and early 70's, I didn't think being black was any obstacle at all. I didn't even know that society thought I was a little different until 1972, when I was 10 years old. We visited Missoula, Montana where dad was doing some graduate work which he did a lot in those days. One of my friends I met asked me quite honestly once, why was my skin so dark, had I stayed in the sun too long? In Montana, during that time-and still today-there were very few black people. I had no answer for his question. I didn't think much about it at the time. Did society have a stigma for me that I didn't know about? I never saw any undo pressure on the face of my father and never did I hear him speak ill of anyone. My mind was filled with the wonderment and curiosity of a child. Although I had seen and heard about racism, my family didn't talk about it very much either. So, I didn't think about it very much. I didn't concern myself with whom I was playing with but only with how much fun I was having.

As a boy, I was not a real good student though I believe I was relatively intelligent. I read all the time, books, newspapers, magazines and anything that was interesting. I especially like the Encyclopedia book with color pictures; they were my favorites. However, my attention span was short on things that I had to concentrate on. I liked to play with my friends during class; it was not popular with the other kids for you to be so smart. They would sometimes ridicule or beat you up.

Mostly, I was shy and didn't have a lot of confidence speaking out. Some people thought I was autistic because they sometimes saw me playing with pencils or crayons like they were basketball men. Inside, I had an active imagination but I knew what reality was. Reality to me was my friends. My best friends were Howard, whom I had known ever since I could remember, and Darrly, who stayed across the street from Howard, Craig, who was a year older than us, Dexter, who moved into our neighborhood in the sixth grade and Lawrence, who later became the unofficial leader of the group. Lawrence moved into the neighborhood in the third grade. He seemed bolder and tougher than the rest of us. At the time, we were surprised he wanted to hang with us. We thought we were not too hip and for him to choose us made us feel good. Lawrence, I think, was glad to settle down from the fast paced and turbulent life style that he had been used to. To him, we were refreshing. He had been around a lot of older kids in his neighborhood and among us felt more experienced.

We all stayed in the southeast section of town in the community of Sunny side, in a middle class black neighborhood named Hillwood. Our homes were built when blacks were just becoming successful and had money. Our families were stable with mothers and fathers at home. Houston, during this time, was booming with opportunity. It was a growing city with good employment possibilities.

Because my father worked in the industry, I heard about the NASA Space Center. Also there were The Chemical and Oil industries and the Medical profession but thinking about those companies as future jobs at that age was not one of my big priorities.

We were idealistic, imaginative kids with a spirit for life. My family consisted of two older brothers and a sister. Abraham Jr. was the oldest; he and my father seemed to have at least one argument a day. Julius was a year younger than Abraham. He was fun loving and worked well with his hands. He was always fixing on something but would sometimes daydream in his own little world. Ann, 4 feet 11 inches tall and weighing only about 98 pounds was very outspoken and feared no one. I was closest to her, although she would play and leave me in a store or somewhere by myself when I was younger. Although they were all born one year apart, they all graduated high school at the same time.

I didn't get to play a lot with my brothers and sister while growing up because they were older and had their own circle of friends. They tried, but they didn't get to teach me a lot about growing up because they didn't have the time. What I learned growing up I learned mostly from the indirect examples set by my peers. Since my parents were older, I didn't think they necessarily understood what I was going through or could remember how it was for them as kids. They grew up in the early thirties and forties and life for blacks had surely changed from their time. With television, fast cars and little legal racism, life was truly faster and more open. Growing up was a constant struggle between the peer pressure of my friends and the values set by my parents. They constantly clashed. My parents tried to instill me with fine moral values. Neither of my parents smoked or drank and they never swore a day in their life that I could remember. They went to religious services every Sunday, though to different services and preached love for your fellow man.

I normally went to service with my mother as my brothers and my sister did. My father would say he was too busy and except for the psychological, would leave the rearing to my mother.

So I initially took her values and followed in her footsteps. My mother was a very religious woman and could be strict. She wanted me to follow the religious and moral values she set forth. On the one hand, my father was a Methodist who took an active role in politics and society. My mother, on the other hand, was a Jehovah's Witness who said she wanted no part of the world. She was also slightly timid and nervous, which I somewhat inherited from her. Often I have found myself wanting to speak out and say or do something but be nervous to act. I began to somewhat resent my lack of self -confidence and began to swear at school and fight like the other boys. I was still, shy but all I wanted was someone to help me open up.

Toward the end of the sixth grade, I became sort of brazen and didn't do my schoolwork. All I was concerned about was having fun and being with my friends. While playing baseball one day, I got into a fight with one of the Dotson brothers. It was instigated by Craig. After he had started calling young Dotson names, he instigated a fight for me with the older Dotson after I called the younger one a name also. The older Dotson was a year older and twelve pounds heavier than I . I was scared and was thinking of whether to fight or run, when he pushed me hard with both hands in the chest. Instantly , I swung back with a left, right combination that dazed the slower Dotson. After grappling with him and throwing a few more well place punches, we were broken up. I remember feeling exuberant and strong walking back home. To beat a boy a year older and twelve pounds heavier put me in a jaunty mood. I thought to myself next time I might not be so lucky. I had lost three fights to the neighborhood bully Darrly Ray. He was not taller than me and not much bigger, but it was something about him that scared me a little. He had an aggressive attitude and reputation. I tried to stay out of his way, whenever I saw him.

When the last day of school came I was ready for it . I got up early and went to Lawrence's house. He was still asleep. I shook him hard but he didn't wake up. I shook him harder and he still didn't wake up. I then took one of his dirty socks off the floor and placed it in front of his nose. He unconsciously swung his hand back and forth, like swinging at a fly. I roared with laughter, waking Lawrence. He got up looking like an angry bull. "Man, why-why you messing wit me?"He moaned. "It's time to get ready for school". I said still laughing a little. It took Lawrence about fifthteen minutes to get ready for school. He was a neat dresser. Lawrence's parents were not rich but they had money. Both were school principals. We left and caught up with Howard and Darrly. We sat on the bridge like we did most mornings just talking. We had been told by Mr. Trotty, a six grade teacher, not to sit on that bridge because a car might come out of control and hit us, but we liked to sit on that bridge anyway. We could see all the action from there. This morning Mr. Trotty saw us. He came out, got us and took us to his room. He said he was going to teach us a lesson once and for all. He showed us his bored but just before he lowered the boom on us he relented. He said some of us were not on that bridge before and he was going to give us another chance. He sent us to our rooms. Before we left he said to us if he ever caught us again on that bridge he would tan our hides and didn't care if we were twenty years old. We never sat on that bridge again.

It almost took me all of class to finally settle down. I counted the final minutes, then school was out. When I got outside I noticed gangs forming on either sides of the bridge. I had heard that Cloverland and Hillwood neighborhoods were going to have a gang fight. I stayed in Hillwood but I hadn't planned to do any fighting today. A girl brushed by me in a blink of an eye; Lawrence was in hot pursuit behind her. I dropped my books and ran after them. The girl was Angela Shannon., who had pestered Lawrence ever since he had come to the school in the third grade. Lawrence was gaining on her quickly. With a last grasp of speed, Angela a block away from her home, ran into her cousin's yard. "You can't come into my cousin's yard", she turned and said huffing and puffing. Not knowing any better we obeyed. Lawrence was dejected. He turned and started towards school. Lawrence's vain in his head was throbbing. He wanted to hit something when it throbbed like that. "I'm still going to get her, she know it". he said as we were walking back to school. He scared me sometimes when he got mad. He would get these fierce looks on his face. The police broke up the gang fight before it started, and told everyone to go home as we got back to school. I picked up my books and we started down the bayou for home.

The start of a brand new world awaited us. We were sentimental and believing kids. We said we were never going to let anyone else be our friend and if they tried we would beat them up. Dreams we had; I wanted to be a writer. I thought writing would give me more time to consider what I wanted to say and I did not have to be confronted by the issue or person I was addressing Since I was shy of speaking out, I felt this could be right up my alley. Novelist were my favorites. I especially liked the way writers such as Irwin Shaw used their imaginations to tell interesting and entertaining stories. I felt this could by my profession. I knew I couldn't be a mathematician like my dad, it just didn't interest me.

In the seventh grade, I went to Johnston Junior High not far from Westbury Square on the southwest side of town. Johnston was a predominantly white school with about two hundred blacks going there at the time. Most of us attended through a minority to majority transfer program which was intended to help integrate blacks more. I decided to go there because I did not want to go to my neighborhood school Woodson. They had a reputation of being wild and fighting a lot. Of all my friends, only Gilbert was going there, and he had a crutch. His older brother attended Woodson and would keep him from being picked on. All of the rest of us intended to go to Johnston, but at the last minute Lawrence and Dexter decided to go to Dowling Junior High, the school Craig attended. He influenced them into it. Howard, Darrly and I originally were the only ones who went to Johnston, but Gilbert ended up coming in the eight grade after his brother graduated from Woodson. From the first day at Johnston I could see it was going to be exciting. The bus ride to school was always interesting. Anything from a rape to gambling could happen on that bus. I sat near the front because only the cool boys or ninth graders would sit in the back.

By the time the last passengers were picked up the seats were full and some people had to stand up. On the last stop a girl named Vanessa would get on. There were no seats so she had to stand up. Unfortunately, one day she was standing with her back towards Howard. He couldn't resist the temptation. He tried to get a quick feel before she knew who did it. However, she was looking out of the corner of her eye. She whirled in one spinning motion and slapped Howard high in the temple. It echoed all over the bus. Later, that same day, when we saw her, she rolled her eyes at Howard but didn't seem to be angry. In fact, she had a smile on her face. Later, they went steady. I did not understand this. I did not understand girls. Around girls I felt uncertain, afraid I would do something inexperienced or stupid. In elementary school, I thought I hated girls. I thought they were unnecessary because all they did was cry and complain. Now I started to see the beauty of girls and came to appreciate them. I had a crush on Shawn, a slim bright complexion girl with long hair in a pony-tail. She wore some cute square glasses that fit her perfectly. She carried herself with elegance and simplicity. I did not like the vulgar show-out type girl. I tried to win Shawn's affection by playing tag, hitting her and running, childish things. For a little girl trying to look and act like a lady, that was out of the question. She would play hard to get and roll her eyes at me. After a while I lost interest; rejection hurt. I did not get over my crush on Shawn until the ninth grade.

My first report card from Johnston presented me with a problem. It had a "P" in conduct on it. My mother always told me I might not be able to do the work, but I could at least be quiet and allow others to learn. I thought about that card all day because I knew what would happen when I got home. I decided not to mention it at all and hope she would not say anything to me about it. As I walked up the driveway I saw an oil spot that had been slashed with water, on it appeared a rainbow. The sun beamed it with illuminated colors. I was fascinated. I thought that since a rainbow is an omen for good things to come, I was going to be all right. I went inside the house and it was.

Being black at Johnston was not really a problem for me. Some blacks felt we were at a school in a school. We would sit by each other at lunch, and mostly, hung out only with each other. We intermingled with the whites occasionally. In classes that were not that strict, we would get a chance to get to know them. There was not much trouble at all. Only one time in three years did someone try to humiliate me on account of my color. Probably only then because he was bigger than I and feared no ret-ribution. There was almost a big gang fight once between the black and white football players. I don't know how it got started, but it was broken up after only a few punches and never arose again. Though there was usu-ally no out and out racism, there was, however, always an unspoken ten-sion that followed us at school. For example, in a class with only three blacks out of twenty five students we could feel the pressure. The teachers at Johnston were good. There were some fine black teachers that provided good role models and some caring white teachers. Some teachers, we could see it in their eyes and in their expressions they felt we were out of their league.

Towards the end of the ninth grade, I had recovered from my rejection from Shawn well enough to have four girlfriends. Two girls that I met at summer school and two at Johnston that somewhat shared me. I was riding high, feeling socially fulfilled. I was coming out of my shyness and felt it was only a matter of time before I reached further heights. Something soon happened that reversed my attitude. I was involved in a gang fight. While riding home from school someone threw some paper out of the bus window at some of the Cloverland boys. These boys went to Woodson and had some of the worst reputations in the neighborhood. They resented us for going to Johnston because they thought we thought we were better than them. They accused me of throwing the paper. I was scared to death. They would use any excuse to pick a fight. Out of the corner of my eye, I could see Lawrence's bus arriving. He would be late getting there. I was on my own for awhile. Finally, after accusing me and pushing me a little, they were ready to leave until Darrly Ray pushed me into one of them. The fight was on, but I couldn't react. For some reason my arms just wouldn't move. I was hit in the face about twelve times before I realized what was happening. Lawrence, whose bus had arrived, came over and tried to help. He had a fight with Darrly Ray before and had clearly dominated him. I saw him knock down about two or three of them, but he couldn't fight them all, there were two many. The fight stopped when I was knocked down the bayou and they got tired of beating on me. I felt disgraced and demoralized. I hadn't even put up a decent fight to help my friend, who went out of his way to help me. I went into a shell, hardly coming out to play with my friends. I went to school and pretty much stayed to myself, though I put on a good front around the girls. I was ashamed. I soon lost my girlfriends, they found out about my little games. I didn't have the zest I once had. My confidence was shattered. I knew it was going to be hard getting it back. However, I was determined to try.

I enrolled in Ross Sterling High School. All my friends were going to a different school except Dexter and I. We were all trying to establish a new independence. Sterling was a predominantly black school on my side of town. It was not the school I was zoned to, which was Worthing High School. The guys I had a fight with were probably going to Worthing, and I did not want to attack my problems direct. Gilbert was going to Worthing, but his brother was attending Worthing also. At Sterling, I tried to establish myself as a cool or hip guy. I started hanging out with people who were skipping class and breaking rules. Eventually, I went further, drinking heavier and barely keeping my grades up. I was headed towards a catastrophe. It soon came. I went on a drinking binge one day and they had to wheel me out unconscience in a wheelchair. Some say I did it just to talk to a girl, but that was an excuse. I mainly did it just to get the extra courage to get through the day. I was at an all time low. I felt ashamed, but not like before. I felt the only place to go was up. I gravely longed for the peer support of my true friends. They had somewhat ostracized me after the gang fight and hearing of my exploits at Sterling but they always kept an interest in what I was doing. I finally realized that though they sometimes talked negative about me, they truly cared about what happened to me. Their genuineness and persistence helped me stay out of trouble. We went off to college together, where we really learned how to give and take with a roommate, how to deal with inner-circle politics and how to feed and amuse ourselves when things were barren. My friends and I still are enduring trials and tribulations, such as fallouts. Nevertheless, we have all practically made it to being successful people in society. We still keep in touch with each other, even though I don't see them often, they know they can count on me if they need me. They played a major part in my maturation. They and many other new friends help me sustain a continuing sense of faith. My experiences as a kid were only slightly more unusual than the next kids. Houston provided a sense of hospitality that should not be underestimated. My neighborhood was proud and humble, many people having stayed in Houston and in Hillwood most of their lives. Houston provided a sense of stability. It was not too fast to make your head spin but fast enough to keep things interesting. With the amount of open land and area in Houston you didn't feel cramped; you felt you could move around. The things that happened to me growing up probably could have happened anywhere, but I might not have been able to pull myself back up elsewhere. In other big cities with fast pace and turbulent life styles, I might have gotten into too much trouble before I even knew what hit me. It probably would have branded me for life. I haven't fulfilled my true potential by any means yet. I am still scurrying to get my chance to achieve. I would like to get more degrees , probably spurred by the awareness of our fine area academic institutions of learning. I had thought that my father had no common sense when I was young, that he was way out of step with what was happening. I finally realized that my father was a survivor. If he could last this long in this periscope, rough world and still be admired and respected by his peers, he was to be applauded. He set a good role model of work, self discipline and education that I'm still trying to live up to. I realized that he is in step and those that can't deal with it are out of step.

Growing up black in Houston was a wonderful experience, through trials and tribulations, there was love and caring that emoted. It taught me that the color of my skin should not be used as a stumble, that the will to succeed must come from my mind and that dignity, self discipline, and character make up the essence of a successful man. People will always try to hold you back no matter what color you are. If I do encounter racism in my pursuits. I must trust in GOD and show those who wish to stop me that I will not be stopped without a struggle. Success in Houston is not easy. In my old neighborhood, I see many guys I grew up with still sitting around on the corner and on the bridge Mr Trotty told us to stay off of. They seem to have no direction, no guidance and no hope for a future better life. They have given up on succeeding and are just surviving day today . Dreams have become a foreign world to them. Many, I remember had great potential to do something in their lives. Every time I see them, they provide me with true motivation and determination because I know we are really not that much different. It was just something in their lives that didn't influence them to achieve or follow rules while I had influences of achievement and right and wrong in my life. I must keep pushing to make sure I don't get trapped in that predicament.

The caring and neighborliness of Black Houstonians and others helped to pull me to where I am today, having a chance to succeed. They helped me to eventually develop social skills and foster a true feeling for my fellowman. I learned a great amount at my part time job as a beer vendor at the Houston Astrodome. I learned to deal one to one with all types of people, from the very nice to the loud and obnoxious. I gained the poise not to get rattled and to be courteous in the face of frivolous provocation. I can still be slightly timid at times, but I have the courage to speak whenever necessary on any subject.

To succeed in Houston, I know I must concentrate and work hard. More or less, Houston today, is a fair town where any person with skill and commitment can achieve. With the fine precedent set by our excellent City Councilman, our former police chief (Now Mayor) and other top administrators, we see that Houston is a place where Blacks can achieve. Back when I was growing up, I guess I might have felt a little subconscious stigma of inferiority because I saw so few Blacks on television or other positive images. I didn't see very much about blacks in school books or any other books I read. However, I always felt I could and would succeed. Nothing or nobody could tell me I couldn't succeed just because I was black. My dreams probably would not have let me listen anyway. When I was growing up I always felt an opportunity would open up. I never can remember seeing signs that said white only. Granted, it was in the early 70's but it was only five or six years after the Civil Rights Movement.

That feeling of opportunity that Houston provided my friends and I with we continue to carry with us today. If we set our minds to it, we know we can achieve our goals.

I would like to travel the world some day but hopefully, I can live the rest of my life in Houston. Houston contains all the things I need and want in my life. Our theaters, sports, social atmosphere and tranquility keeps our lives interesting and fulfilling. My goal is to become a writer and I am going to keep shooting for that goal no matter what anyone else says until I run out of bullets, then I will use my fist. Many times in my life I've tried to run away from situations that felt uncomfortable. If there is one thing I have learned in my life, it is you can never run away from the fight or the fighters. Wherever you go the fight will always follow you. That same fight is everywhere because people are people wherever you go. Until you stand up to it, it will always keep you running. If you stay running you can't establish yourself firmly and you won't be on solid ground. But when I talk about fighting I'm not talking about fighting with your fist; I talking about fighting with your heart and soul. We all have this ability to fight . The fighter that you must overcome is in you. This is the fighter that is holding you back. He is the only fighter you can totally control. Put all of your energy into improving yourself and the rest will come.

If you can do these things and stay away from some of the tribulations that can obstruct success, you have about as good of a chance as I do. No matter what color you are, you can always achieve your goal.

BABY WARRIORS

A second grade student at the school where I worked said to me, "I'm going to kill myself; I'm dumb". For all my trying I could not get him to say I can; I'm a good person. Tommy had many reasons for low self esteem. His background was low social economic. The apartments he stayed in were drug infested and deteriorating; they were not far from the school he attended. What he saw everyday were pushers, drug dealers, and hustlers; that didn't give him much hope. His mother was in prison, so Tommy stayed with his aunt. She already had four kids of her own. Whereabouts of his father were unknown. The effect of this family situation became apparent later.

A teacher and I went to Tommy's house to get special permission from his aunt for Tommy to get a hearing device he needed for class. The apartment was small and plain, not many extravagances. It wasn't really dirty but kind of drab. The apartment had a well worn look about it. Tommy's aunt seemed relatively glad to see us. She seemed glad someone was taking an interest in Tommy. Every now and then he would peak around the hallway corridor wall. He was uncomfortable. Tommy's aunt told us his mother was still away at prison and she didn't know when she was coming back. She said she had four kids of her own but did what she could for Tommy. We told her we understood. It must have been difficult for her to raise another child when it was hard enough to raise her own children.

However, I sensed something else. I sensed that she felt put upon by the extra burden and that Tommy felt this indifference also. At school, Tommy had a hostile attitude. His clothes were unkept, many times smelling of urine. His hair was usually in knots and many times dirty. Tommy would get into a lot of fights because the other kids would tease him. Everyday, I could see him withdrawing more and more. He wanted and needed attention but didn't feel there was anyone one he could trust. His frustration came to a boil with him threatening to commit suicide. He told me (I hope) because he trusted me. He said it to get attention but the mere fact that he said it meant he was thinking about it. Tommy was crying out to the world. He is typical of many lower income, inner city minority youth.

Tommy is like many other children, feeling the hopelessness of the unloved and the indifference of the uninvolved and he is giving up. When I was in the second grade I didn't know what suicide was. I probably would have thought it was some kind of soft drink or something. Someone has repeated in Tommy's ear and preached to him in his heart that he is not worthy. He is told he is not good enough and that he is dumb by society.

He is caught up in a jagged existence, ridiculed and unwanted in his social environment and treated with disdain and indifference in his home. In his peer world, he is laughed and scoffed at by unsensitive kids who care too much about what he has on and about how much money he has but not about him as a person. He doesn't have the clothes or social attire to make him feel accepted nor does he have the academic understanding to help him get self esteem that way. At no front can Tommy find a positive measure of self worth. No wonder he is bitter and ready to curse the world. His little mind has not been given the tools to survive in life, much less in school. The system fails him by placing an emphasis upon a product instead of the producer, and by placing emphasis upon statistics instead of the spirit of the child. Tommy needs a different direction.

Tommy needs to be instilled with a competitive, fighting spirit to enable him to attain a positive sense of self.

All children must be told and instilled under the old adage: You don't get something for nothing. They must be made aware to the realities and the difficulties of life. Children must be taught early, that although they are not in control of their lives now, ultimately they, and only they, will be responsible for it. They must be taught; they must be strong and fight a battle like someone was trying to take food out of their mouth. They must be prepared for the bitter world in which we live and not have its existence sugar coated to them. What Tommy needs is a repetition of positive reinforcement. He needs to find some task or game that he can excel in. After he has mastered these skills, he can move on to new, more challenging task he can accomplish, while receiving help and encouragement. Tommy's mind and learning capabilities are as good as anyone else. The problems Tommy encountered are typical of the youth of today. Many do not understand what is expected of them. They are not accepted in their peer group nor do they find comfort in the academic setting. They start believing that they can't achieve. Unless they learn to believe in themselves they will not receive the benefit of an education.

Students have lost that intangible that students used to have. There is a big difference between the youth of today and the youth of yesterday. Our fathers and forefathers knew you had to work hard for what you got. They listened to their elders and had great respect for authority. They believed in working for a goal and didn't expect something for nothing. Today's youth are impatient and materialistic. Many believe that material things make you who you are and a lot of them will do anything to get the things they want. They have no respect for authority or for their fellowman. They are constantly trying to beat the system and find the easy way out. This is a different world students must learn in today.

Society has changed from the day of our forefathers. Life is faster, more complex and more dangerous today. Children are exposed to more by the age of 10 that children would have been exposed to formerly by age 30.

Television and media show images of glamour, but they don't emphasize the hard work it takes to attain that glamour. Society paints a picture that it is easy to be a success, that anyone can do anything they want. This is just not true. When children start dealing with reality and finding out it is not easy; they become extremely frustrated. Little Tommy was facing that frustration. On the other hand he had not been given the tools for success. He did not have a stable home environment. He was not receiving positive reinforcement. And most importantly, he did not have a clear understanding of what he was up against. He could not see any hope out of his situation. Tommy did not care about living because he felt he didn't have anything to live for. Society tells him to love and be fair when in reality life can very cruel and unfair. The television he watches has every story finishing in a happy ending with the good guy winning. However, he sees the ugly realities of the nightmares, with the good guy —if he can recognize the difference between them— not always winning. Students become frustrated with adults telling them one thing when another situation truly exist. They can see through the hypocrisy and what they see does not look good to them. They see a society that says education is very important but sends a mixed message by exalting athletes and entertainers showering them with praise and rewards while sending only a trickle down to education. Students are no different than any of us. They need food and shelter, a sense of security, a feeling of belonging and love. If any of these necessities are lacking, it can severely hamper their self esteem. It is very hard for a child to care about learning when they don't care about themselves.

However, there is still a chance for Tommy.

Positive reinforcement and repetition could reverse the negative stigma that this student carries with him. A network system of people who care could provide this reinforcement. Anybody from the corner store checker to the neighborhood police officer could serve as positive role models. We must get children involved in better peer groups at an early age. The cub scouts, boy scouts, girl scouts, little league football and baseball, etc., are all positive and constructive avenues for kids to vent their energy, and keep their competitive fire burning. We also need to introduce students to other competitive pursuits that will exercise their mind. Let's start school chess clubs, spelling contest, and business carnivals. Children must learn early that there is a direct correlation between using mind and making money.

Education is at an all time low. Students see us more concerned about whether they score a touchdown or win a beauty contest than whether they will get an "A" or a "B". Students will do whatever will get more attention. If they receive more attention by playing football, or by having fancy clothes, or having a fancy car then so be it; that's what they will work for. They will do whatever it takes to get the attention they need, even if it means saying they are going to commit suicide. We must teach students to fight with their mind and spirit as early as possible. We must raise baby warriors. If we want students to act right and study, then we have to give them the attention they need for appropriate behavior and good grades. As long as they get the attention for what they do that's good, students will keep doing it. If they don't receive attention for what they do that is good, that is when students like Tommy start crying out for attention anyway they can.

This is a true story but some of the names and situations have been changed.

THE FIRST IS NOT THAT WHICH IS PHYSICAL

As Humans we are sometimes a peculiar species. Look around at other living forms. From what we know other life forms have no such ritual as marriage. They don't particition off and say only we two animals or us two plants are going to stick together and try to survive. Fish and Plants reproduce asexually, through a process of photo synthesis of sunlight and water. They don't have to join in any physical action , they just have to be. Mammals, a warm blooded species, reproduce through sexual inter-course. The method by which they do this is sometimes humorous by our standards as humans. However, Animals understand about survival. The difference between we as humans and animals is many times we care more about a false sense of pride and status than survival.

When we are looking for marriage mates we tend to concentrate on the superficial as opposed to the practical. We liken our marriage to a fantasy fairytale; We want to find true love and live happily ever after.

The reality is 1 out of every 2 marriages ends in divorce. The biggest reason couples give for breaking up is money problems, lack of communication and infidelity. One of the biggest problems is when individuals look for a relation-ship, they look for the wrong factors.

51

Most people get caught into looking at the physical aspects of a person without having a full understanding of what that person is like inside. Are they selfish? Do they live up to their word? Do they have a bad temper? Will they really love you when times get bad.

The ultimate goal of any relationship is survival and growth. In American relationships we put too much emphasis on a perfect nuclear family. One man and woman pledging to love each other forever and promising to raise a family and deal with all problems by themselves. Many times the demands of life are too great even for couples that sincerely love each other.

In many international countries relationships have a more practical goal of survival for a common purpose instead of some sort fantasy or fairy-tale. Their common purpose is survival of the group. In many countries and communities, couples are pledged together by their families, many times without the two people never having met. What is best for the two family groups is more paramount than individual desires of the two people involved. Wars have been halted or averted by unions of planned marriages. In some communities a male may have as many marriage partners as he chooses if he a can take care of them. The more marriage partners you can take care of the greater esteem you receive from society. We look upon this as despicable in this country. How can one man truly love all his partners and be living right in the name of GOD. But I ask how many women wouldn't mind sharing Michael Jordan if they could; he certainly can afford to take care of more than one mate.

We remember throughout the bible Abraham, Lot, Solomon and many other bible figures had numerous marriage partners. And down through history many successful communities have had multiple marriage or relationship partners as a part of their normal society. In America with our spiraling upward divorce rate and our increasing sexual crimes of rape and child molestation. Maybe we should look at different ways of having relationships with each other. Sharing should be okay with proper medical attention if the needs of the family can be progressed. The worst thing is not sharing a mate or having a planned marriage but worse is to not having anyone to help you in this overwhelming world .

Everywhere you look there are springing up new cabarets, nude clubs and X-rated massage parlors.

In this day and age it seems people are getting further and further away from satisfying sexual relationships.

It is almost as if people have become a meat market of sexual exploitation. People are unsatisfied sexually and are seeking. How important is sex to a person's healthy self esteem and confidence. How are those incapacitated or unable to engage in sexual intercourse able to survive without going crazy? For most of us, we are constantly saddled with urges. If we are unable to ventilate or control our urges it could cause a neurosis in the mind. How can a person live an entire lifetime without ever engaging in sex? What is the secret?

There is something much deeper which gives a much greater feeling of ecstasy than sexual intercourse.

Everyone living is seeking something. Even if its only to wake up and live another day. Sex is an extra pleasure. It is included in the human being and made to feel good so that humans would be encouraged to procreate and multiply.

Many of us get sidetracked to look at sex as a means to an end. The ultimate accomplishment. Our children have suffered the consequences of this type of vision. During slavery and segregation young boys felt a bond to protect and help the girls as much as they could. The boys extended family included his sisters, aunts, great aunts, grandmothers and many times even great grandmothers. Boys developed a reverence for the woman in their family and would not dream of treating them in a disrespectful or abusive way. This tradition changed with integration and the new directions in the black community. There became a competing atmosphere between young boys and girls. Boys began to look at young girls as beings to be conquered and played with not as equal partners.

Sex is a quick and instant gratification. By itself its lasting effects are minimal. I don't care how beautiful and good looking your partner is, if all you have together in common is sex you will get tired of them. They will seize to be satisfying and will become like flesh to you.

The concept of building trust, friendship and love takes too long for many of us. This is one of the reasons why friendship is one of the pre-requisites to a satisfying relationship. When you've laughed together, played together and worked on issues together its much easier to build a trusting relationship.

Our fleshly bodies are mere shells for our inner being. Many times we've seen individuals who have the makeup to be very attractive but because of how they live and how they feel they look horrible; like someone you wouldn't wish to be near. At the same time we've seen individuals who didn't have what appeared to be any special attractiveness but carried an air of beauty and dignity that transcended their physical makeup.

Our spirit carries us, it shapes us. How we use our spirit determines who are. Our natural inclination is to live spiritually but our understanding of life is physical. For us the first is that which is physical or fleshly. We still seek to satisfy our physical urges first. We seek gluttony of food. We seek to drink to overflow the pallet. We seek quick laughs and fast fun. There are historical reason for this which I will not go into now. But in sex for the most part we seek instant gratification to satisfy our ego. *Sex allows a quick fix of our urges but without love it damages our spirit. The closer we get to a loving relationship the closer we are to a connection with the creator.*

The Rise of Sexually Explicit businesses is because people are seeking an excitement and stimulation of their senses and inner being and also in some cases a release from the pressures of life. They are seeking another touch, another impulse that may respark the embers of their soul even if only for a day. What we are all ultimately seeking is a much higher feeling of ecstasy. Part of Jesus mission and ability was to look beyond the physical makeup of an individual and to look at their heart. His examples of the good Samaritan by the road, the example of Canaanite woman who wished her daughter to be healed and the woman caught in adultery show Jesus was less concerned with physical limits and labels but more concerned with the feelings and actions of the individual.

Man in his limited wisdom sees everything in the physical realm. He sees with his appetite; he desires and wants what he sees. However, all around man is the spiritual realm. Our blocks and our inequalities hinder our vision to see spiritually. As we grow more and seek GOD, we gain the ability to see more spiritually. The first understanding of man is not that which is spiritual but that which physical. When a baby first comes out of the womb and starts to grow, they cry for milk or because they have a dirty diaper. Later they begin to realize they have a greater power. A child begins to see the wonders of the universe and realizes that he or she is connected to a higher power and in time they seek to understand that power. We are born with a desire and longing to seek a connection with this higher power.

The scripture says " GOD is Love, Whoever lives in love lives in GOD and GOD in him". This is the relationship I am seeking and which I'm still a long way from. I have delved into sin many times to know what darkness feels like but GOD has continued to let me have a small light of hope that one day I may find this greatest love. The greatest love is to have a connection to the creative force that permeates the universe and to

be one with another's human beings soul . This is the greatest love that
we all are seeking.

A handicapped person with no arms or legs still has the spirit of life
inside of them. They do not need sexual intercourse to keep them going.
They have learned to connect with an inner being and an inner love
inside them that lifts them above the limitation of sexual stimulation.

Don't get me wrong sex is beautiful. It is joyous and great. Its greatest
purpose is the miracle of life it creates but to not be able to engage in it
would not be the end of the world. Never pity those incapacitated or
unable to engage in sex again. If they are surviving maybe they have
found something within themselves that gives a them a much greater
feeling than sexual intercourse ever could.
Maybe they have found that greatest love that all of us are seeking and it
is the key to their survival. If we had more of that spirit inside of us
maybe we could live better also.

A LETTER TO A FRIEND: TRYING TO CATCH UP WITH MYSELF

Hello. How are you doing? I hope fine. Life is too short to hold a grudge. Smile. I enjoy writing, so if it's not too much of a bother I'd like to continue. Sometimes the skills GOD has blessed me with get me into trouble. He gave me a photographic memory. Many people put too much stock into my remembering or knowing something about them when it comes naturally to me. What's been going on? Work is going fine. I'll be glad when the Christmas break comes I may go to Atlanta for vacation.

We never really got to talk about the Farrakhan program. I agreed 99% with what he was saying at the program. He is very right about one thing. If we harp upon divisions between religious idealogies or Greek organizations, we will be stuck in a stagnated state of small mindedness. We must look at people as individual human beings. One is no better than the other. However, he didn't go into the philosophy upon which the Nation of Islam is based. He didn't talk about their belief that Mr. Yacub, a big headed scientist in Mecca, raised up a devil race of white skin people to conquer and enslave the controlling black race. It is taught, that Mr. Yacub was angry because the people of Mecca exiled him and 59,999 followers on the island of Patmos. Mr. Yacub had people with recessive gene structures to separate from each other the two genes, black and brown, and then graft the brown gene to progressively lighter, weaker stages. The resulting humans would be, as they became lighter and weaker, progressively more susceptible to wickedness and evil. Only brown and brown or black and brown were permitted to marry. Black babies were killed. Mr. Yacub left rules to follow after he died. Finally over 800 years, the blacks were changed to brown, to red, to yellow and then finally to white. This white bred race came back to the mainland, and started telling lies and disrupting the peace. They were exiled again to caves in Europe, where they stayed until Moses rescued them. It is taught the books of Moses in the caves are missing from the bible. Then it's said the white race would rule the world for six thousand years until from the black race would rise one with infinite power. It is also taught GOD came to earth in the 30's posing as a seller of silk named W.D. Fard to teach and lead black people. After setting up the Nation of Islam, Master W.D. Fard mysteriously vanished, leaving the Nation to the leadership of Elijah Muhammad. Elijah, it is taught, was the second coming of Christ. He emphasized as does Farrakhan that blacks are GOD's chosen people. (Reference " The Autobiography of Malcolm X", by Alex Haley)

I have no problem with saying Jesus was black; if you look at his ancient lineage, it's quite possible because he is related to people of color. What I have a problem with is saying that one color is better than another. Jesus could have been any color and it wouldn't matter because he was spiritual. We are judged by what we do, not by the color of our skin, our size or our religious title. As black people, our biggest mistakes come from trying to copy or be just like whites. Our greatest accomplishments have come when we have followed a spiritual path. I believe GOD looks at our hearts; to him there is no color, title or size to him. Those that do GOD's will are his children. Choosing a people on the basis of color would be Calvinistic or predestination, there would be no hope. I believe everyone has an equal chance to serve GOD. Farrakhan certainly was right when he said black men are under siege but we are under siege not only from the white community— that's always been— but also we are under siege from the community at large. I've had many black people who tried to disrespect me because I am black and young. People live in stereotypes and the black man is placed at the lowest end of it. Unless a black man is an athlete, entertainer, or known as brilliant, he is going to encounter it. Our fathers and grandfathers encountered it but they knew what they were up against. They conditioned themselves everyday to deal with it. Our forefathers didn't have the opportunity we have today so they didn't set their hopes too high. They were happy with the small successes they made, one step at a time.

Today we don't understand the struggle we are spoiled. We got where we are through spiritual sacrifice. I understand about being spoiled. I was extremely sheltered growing up and I still am sometimes. I can't tell you how many times my father has bailed me out of situations. He's been my rock; without him I would not be able to continue my struggle today. Most problems I've had in my life come from that aspect of my upbringing. I know to spoil a child, especially a black boy, is one of the worst things you can do to him(short of physical harm). Spoiling him makes him handicapped to dealing with the realities of life. Once he gets out into the real world they won't spoil him; he will have to deal with its realities. If he is ill equipped, he will fall by the wayside. That's what happens to many young men. What we lost is the struggle, the sacrifice. Most people are only concerned about getting what they want not about doing what is right. Children are going wrong because they don't know which way to turn. There's so much pressure on them. We tell them to wait and be patient, yet we treat them as if they don't matter because they're young and don't own any material possessions. Everybody wants to be a somebody.

Our natural inclination is to live spiritually. Watch a young child, they are naturally loving. The older and more "mature" they get, more the capacity for evil comes in their heart. It's very hard to live spiritually today. Constantly we are being tempted to do wrong. We just try to take things one step at a time and pray to GOD they keep us moving forward. Fleshly or carnal people see only with their eyes; spiritual people see with their hearts. Combine the two and there's bound to be friction. Sometimes I feel like there's no one really trying to live spiritually, no one I can trust. It gets very lonely and scary. Seems like only those who don't care about doing GOD's will have all the power. People care more about this game or that than whether this baby has enough milk. Priorities are totally out of wack. I carry inside me fear and anxieties all the time from dealing with this type of system. I get so scared sometimes I cry. But I know I must continue to face these situations and find the courage and insight to overcome them. I know I can never totally give in to this system. If I give in I have no chance. Most people are living against GOD's will and I refuse to go along with their standards. There is no difference between any of us. Like Janet Jackson says on her album "In complete darkness we are all the same, it is only our knowledge and wisdom that separates us. Don't let your eyes deceive you".

Our essence is spiritual. Deep inside we are all the same; we just have different shells. I refused to be stereotyped as less than anyone. It's like racism, when, because of our color, they tried to say we were less than human beings, less than men and women. None of us knows the future, there are no guarantees, all we have is GOD's word. I see nowhere in GOD's word where he say's one is better than another, whether black or white, tall or short, fat or skinny. All we have is a heart to GOD. No matter how big or tall we are, an accident can disfigure us. No matter how confident we are, we can find a situation that can shatter our confidence. Our existence is fragile but no matter who we are we have spirit inside of us, no more or no less than anyone else. How we use it determines who we are. A handicapped person with no arms or legs still has the spirit of life inside of them. Inside they are still alive. If something happened to your outer shell you would still have your spirit inside of you.

This is the spirit of GOD's love.

If we ever doubt our spiritual nature or the existence of GOD, all we have to do is ask how did we get here. The state board is having a debate on evolution and creation. Anyone who talks to me about evolution I ask, if we evolved from monkeys how did the monkeys first get here? If they say monkeys were formed out of rock and volcano, I ask how did the rock and volcano get here and so on. Anything they say I point to the fact that some supreme being worked to create a beginning. We can look at all the wonders of the earth, how they work in perfect order and have faith that GOD exist. But what is our purpose? What our we suppose to be doing? Is it only tied to materialism and wants, where the only purpose is to make sure you are better and have more things than the next person? GOD's purpose must be better than that. It must be greater!

We can't see GOD but we can feel Him. Is GOD physically big or small? Is he black or white? Can GOD really be limited by our small mindedness? He is unseen but He is the most powerful in all the earth. Ask old ones, ask the blind, ask the handicapped, ask anyone what is really most important deep down and they'll say love. GOD is love, when we find love we find GOD. I believe He wishes we show as many people as possible how to love with their hearts, minds and souls. I believe He wants us to use our energies to fight for his glory. The rewards that we see before our eyes are minuscule compared to His rewards. The glory of His love should be our goal. I believe GOD's spirit works through all of us from time to time. He is there in our subconscience reminding us of what is right even while we are doing wrong. Our fight is for us to do what is right deep inside of our heart. This is the greatest goal for me.

Friend, I hope our squabbles are behind us. You're a special friend for me. What you say affects me because I think so highly of you. You're a good person; I love the person you are. I'm a man of feeling. If I don't feel it in my heart I can't give my all. What I said was how I felt at the time. I know I'm a difficult man to get along with. I am complex and moody. One day I'd like to learn to love. I want to express myself through my writing and my work. I want to catch up with the best part of myself and seek GOD and do his will. They say we only use one tenth of our brain power. Could you imagine if we used all of our power? We could get to the highest level of our spirit. There is no love greater than spiritual love. There is nothing more powerful, its touch, its feel, can move mountains. I want to thank you for inspiring me to be a better person. I had become disgruntled with the evilness of people. It is refreshing to know that there are some wonderful people out there like you. Take care of yourself and keep a smile.

THE CHRISTALIZATION OF TUPAC SHAKUR
(A LETTER TO MY SON)

What's up J.W. just thought I let you know the pulse of what's happening. We are doing well. I have been able to reset all my stuff I had before the break in. (Computer ,TV, etc.)

It may be a little better now than before. We now have DVD and a 17 inch monitor instead of a 15 inch monitor, I've already watched The Cell and Shaft.

Your mother and I are beginning to mature together, I believe. It takes time. It helps to more appreciate the level of vision that Tupac Shakur had achieved already in his short life and the apparent mistakes he made. In his classic" Dear Momma", Pac explores the dictomy of loving someone and feeling the continual pain of disappointment from that person. When we are young it is very hard to see the pressures that our parents and love ones go through. The friction Tupac went through with his mother caused him to be kicked out of the house. He had difficulty seeing the pain and pressures his mother was going through. Most are familiar with Tupac's difficult upbringing under his mother, who was a former member of the Black Panthers and a crack cocaine abuser. Not the best environment to be raised in but look what a jewel of talent it produced. By the age of twenty five he accomplished what most of us don't accomplish in a lifetime. He produced five albums and many collaborations with other artist which are still being heard till this day. He appeared in five motion pictures with significant scene stealing roles. However, he also had been shot five times, arrested eight times and served almost a year in jail. Tupac's life illuminates the paradox of living as a young black in a world with immense talent where the overall world structure works to tear you down not only through it's structure but mostly through the lessons it teaches us.

It teaches through television that life is always fair and ends in a happy ending. In school it teaches a very incomplete history from only one perspective, that of the western doctrine of "Manifest Destiny".

The images from TV and movies represent a certain type of behavior that is glorified and vilified at the same time. Gangsta Rap is the pulse of the street, the message of reality of unfulfilled hope. Tupac was a leading spokesman of this unfulfilled hope.

I don't mind Jalen my 3 year old son listening at Rap if it has a meaningful message. Not all of Tupac's words had meaningful messages some were just ego tripping but in the direction he was leading his understanding was growing. He has an interesting song on *The Still I Rise* album called Black Jesus. In it he says, *"Cops patrol the projects, hate the people living in them, I was born an inmate waiting to escape the prison. Went to Church but don't understand it, they underhand it, GOD gave me these commandments, the world is scandalous. Blast till they holy high, Baptist they're evil minds. Wise no longer blinded, Watch me shine trick which one of yall want to feel the degrees? Bitches freeze when they face Black Jesus"* Some people might just disregard these words because of the language and believe these are the nonsense ravings of one of those young gangsta rappers who have no societal redeeming qualities. But these words and those of other Rappers like Nelly and Too Short are influencing are society and our children and it is important to know what they are saying.

Tupac was saying that although he was born in a very tough situation he can still achieve because GOD flows through him also. Despite the bravado of the manner of which he says it he is trying to give inspiration to those listening. He goes on to say in the chorus, *"The Pressure knows indefinite fail, some missing souls turn to hoes when exposed to jail, In times of war we need somebody raw, who can rally the troops, like a saint we can trust to help carry us through".*

Tupac understood the odds he was up against everyday as a young black male and wanted to try to inspire with his forum of entertainment. Although some things have changed, the bottom line of survival as a young black male has not. The stereotype still exist that you are a menace to society with only a few exceptions.

What is needed is for those like myself to discipline ourselves and create a legacy for those who come after us. It is a continual process of growth. The pressures of this world affect us in many different ways. I know our lives seem like insanity sometimes. Your mother and I have been through many struggles in our self development and we have both thought about giving up but something keeps us together still. We realize that GOD put us together for a purpose and gave us the gifts we have. So we keep fighting and keep trying.

One thing I realize is no matter how talented we are or how strong we think we are, we cannot achieve lasting success by ourselves. We must be part of a foundation. This is why the Shrine is still very important to us. We still must respect the overall goals of the church even if we have problems with the leadership. They are not perfect, I believe they understand that. But we need each other. We need to be part of a foundation whose stated purpose is the liberation of our people in relationship with GOD. I believe over time we can get past the pain of the disappointment we have felt to help the church live up to its purpose as well as fill our spiritual longing. This is my goal. This is what I will work toward.

You may hear sometimes from the family that I am not being right, not a good influence or other unflattering words. I assure you this is not the case. As a father it is my responsibility to make sure that Jalen has a foundation and understanding of what he is up against and knows a path to follow. No emotionalism or sentimentality can be allowed to infringe upon that responsibility because someone does like the way I do something. What they like is irrelevant, that responsibility was given to me by GOD. Emotionalism and sentimentality are irrelevant, watch the flowers bloom. Sometimes I look ragged, sometimes your mother may be irrational, that's why I believe GOD put us together to find balance. It is our mission to help manifest that balance and foundation in Jalen and Janiya. We constantly fight to shine that light in ourselves and help it shine in others.

Tupac says "It Ain't Easy" and its not you have to stay focused. As he says in "Still I Rise", we are always in a constant struggle. It is a miracle if we make it. Black people have had a hard struggle to go through. We have survived the Middle Passage. We survived slavery. We have survived Jim Crow Laws and oppression. We survive the psychological effects these struggles have caused. The beginning prayer in "Still I Rise" says *"Dear Lord, As were down here struggling for as long as we know, In search for a paradise. Dreams are dreams and reality seems to be the only way to go. The only place for us, I know. Trying to make the best of a bad situation seems to be my life story. Ain't no glory in pain. A soldiers story in vain and can't nobody live this for me. It's a ride yall a long hard ride".* The Cornerstone of our heart is still rising. We continue to survive today and Still We Rise.

The second annual conference was held in Oakland, June 26, 2000 to explore the teachings and writings of Tupac Shakur. The life and legacy of Tupac Shakur become more clear everyday. He did many things in his short life we would not want to role model. But he was a survivor and rebel who cursed at the hypocrisy and inequities in the world and he made sure we heard him. In his recently published book "The Rose That Grew From Concrete", He asked *"Did you hear about the rose that grew from concrete. Proving natural laws wrong it learned to walk without having feet. Funny it seems but by keeping its dreams it learned to breath fresh air. Long live the rose that grew from concrete when no one else even cared"*. We care Tupac. Let all our roses grow.

MELODIES OF A WRITER

"Melodies of a Writer" is the first of many installments of writer Carl Louis Alexander. These lyrical poems were written to be sung to music. They are the total origination of Carl Alexander and are intended to be used for both commercial and poetic purposes.

The lyrics were written in many different song mediums and tempos. The suggested medium and artist appear in the top left corner.

"LIFE AIN'T AS HARD AS IT SEEMS"

1. Group
    Pop
    Medium

You can't be scared, cause if your gonna do it.
Then braveries your friend, there is nothing to it.
Not as hard as it seems, you just got to get to it.

REFRAIN
It might look bleak, You might be shy but it'll turn out better, just you give a try.

CHORUS
Life ain't as hard as it seems, all you need is your dreams.
You will make it if you want to, but you have got to work hard to do.

Nobody will, give you something for nothing.
But you can make it still, if you're really wanting.
You must believe, that you can really do it.
Don't let em try deceive, they'd hope you never knew it.

REFRAIN
CHORUS -Adlib
CHORUS-Adlib

END

"IF I WASN'T A STAR WOULD YOU STILL LOVE ME"

2. Male
   Country
   Slow/Med

I've noticed the way you like my Cadillac,
The clothes I put you in makes your eyes glee.
Never before have you ordered a beer instead of champagne, Sometimes I
wonder girl if I wasn't a star would ya still love me.

CHORUS
*If I wasn't a star would you still love me, would you care for me and comfort
me if this me wasn't what you see.*

*If I didn't have my money and my cars, is it really true that our love would not
go far.*

REPEAT CHORUS
I'm not saying that in your own way you don't love me,
I think that over the years you've learned to care.

But I think that through convenience you've learned to love,
Oh well that's better than if there was never no love at all there.

CHORUS
Repeat CHORUS
Repeat CHORUS
Repeat CHORUS

(2) Could you truly say Girl that things would still be the same.

FADE

"I'll EAT WHAT I HAVE TO EAT (TO SURVIVE)"

3. Group

People think of eating in two very different ways, one is through your mouth and one is a whole nother way.
Eating means doing what you must even though we sometimes feel like fools.

REFRAIN 1
I'll eat what I have to eat to survive.
Cause if you don't eat sometimes you will starve.
REFRAIN 2
Every bodies eaten something they didn't want, But they ate'em any way to survive till they got to their point.

CHORUS 1
Do you eat what you have to eat to survive?
I eat what I have to eat and I'm still alive.

Just when you think if you eat anymore you'll be stuffed,
Time seems to tell you that you have eaten enough.
All eating has to do with is pride, even though I know some of you thought about the lower kind.

REFRAIN 3
I'll eat what I have to eat to survive, if you don't eat sometimes you can't stay alive.
REFRAIN 2,   CHORUS 1

Pressure sometimes makes you want to give in,
But if you eat that pressure in the end remember you will win.

REFRAIN 4
I eat what I have to eat to survive.
Do you eat what you have to eat to stay alive.
I eat what I have to eat to survive,
And despite my eating I'm doing just fine.

CHORUS 1, REFRAIN 1, CHORUS 1, REFRAIN 1, REFRAIN 2

FADE

THE BIRD IN THE PAINTING

4. Male group
   Pop
   Slow Med.

Sometimes somethings just won't let you be free.
It seems our obstacles never end.
Everything seems to come back to how much money we have.
Will things ever be like He intends………………..

REFRAIN 1
Like the bird in the painting who wants to be free.
His canvas is holding back his life.
He might have the whole wide world to see.
But he wasn't born with a silver spoon or knife.
CHORUS 1
Let em fly, let em reach his destiny.
Let em soar the clouds and be all he can be.
Let em fly, fly high upon the sky.
Until we hear his cry…..

The bird in the painting knows he has wings.
But the master of the frame is waiting to have them clipped.
The bird hopes you hear the sad song that he sings.
He wants to reach to heavens tip.

REFRAIN 2
The bird in the painting wants to be free.
The canvas he's in is holding back, (Its holding back his life)…….
We never know what he could one day be.
Until he has his life.

CHORUS 2
(Let em fly)... The bird in the painting wants to be free.
He wants the canvas freed from his life. All he wants is a chance to really be.
He wants to have his pride.

REFRAIN 2, CHORUS 2, (3) Let em fly, let em be free, Let em fly and reach his destiny. CHORUS 2 (repeat)

FADE

"I GOT HIGH HOPES"
(I Believe in Me)

5. Rap
   Male
   Med.

Girl, I know what I'm talking about. Believe in who I am and I'll set you out.
I know you've never heard a man like me before, but listen to me baby, I'll give you more.

REFRAIN 1
See I've got them high hopes, I will soon be there.
Just come with me baby and together we will share.
CHORUS 1
Cause I believe in me yea.   Soon the world will see.

It may be hard for you to right now visualize,
But although I'm down now I'll soon be up high.

You gotta believe.......!

CHORUS 2
I know what I'm doing. I do it right.
Girl you and me together we'll reach new heights. Cause I believe.

I know people are always talking in your ear, Saying I hope, I wish, I could but never getting there.
But don't you know the difference between what is fake and true.
Girl I'm getting where I'm going and I want to go with you.

REFRAIN 1, CHORUS 1, CHORUS 2

Girl believe in me and soon you'll see, All your dreams and all your fantasies.

They'll come to life right before your eyes, when you take me, take as your winning prize.

You may not understand all that I do but girl just remember it's all done for you.

CHORUS 2
(See) Girl You may think me crazy or wildly insane but lady I'm just a man trying to take you to his fame.
REFRAIN 1
I believe, please believe, we can achieve.
(3) I believe in me, I believe in you.
I have enough confidence for two, girl it will be easy if you believe too. I believe.

FADE

"DREAMING"

6. Pop   Male   Med

Falling asleep is what I love, what a special place to be.
You're the girl that I dream of, imagining you is my exclusive treat.
I dream my dream will come true, It's part of the breath I breathe.
You know my dreams to be with you, girl our dream is rated ecstasy.

CHORUS 1
I be dreaming, dreaming of love
I be dreaming, Girl it's you that I dream of.
I be dreaming, dreaming of you
I be dreaming, dreaming of the things we could do.

Dreams can sometimes cause you pain, make you mess your sheets.
But you can't replace the pleasure gain, one night of your love would last
me weeks. Yea maybe you have the same dream too that would be so sweet
then we could get together me and you, we'd make our dreams complete.

CHORUS 1
(4) I be dreaming........
Girl I be dreaming........
Chorus 1

FADE

"CHICKEN"

7. Female RB Up

What's the matter honey? Did I get too close to you.
Did I make you feel uncomfortable and not know what to do. I couldn't
figure it out. You had me wondering was it something wrong with me. But
then I realized I'm not to blame because you're to blind to see.

CHORUS 1
(2) You're Chicken, Bach bach a bach bach bach
You're chicken of my love and it sure is a shame.
REFRAIN 1
You are intimidated. You can't deal with what I represent
I am strong and intelligent, you're scared I may end up president.
And I don't want that incident, so you start feeding me this precedent.

CHORUS 1, REFRAIN 1, CHORUS 1,

FADE

"IT DON'T HAVE TO BE PERFECT" (JUST GOOD)

8. Male   RB   UP

Baby love is like a light bulb as long as you can see
cause it really doesn't matter how bright it's supposed to be.
Satisfaction is all that you need and if we really want to work it then we
will succeed.

Chorus 1

It don't have to be perfect baby (just good).
We don't have to be tens but we could.
You will like my love girl- I know. It will be perfect for you It'll show.
If you're waiting for a dream, then dream on.
But I will make your dreams be gone.
Girl my passion and my fire they are number one. And before you and I
are finished you'll know that love is what you've won.

CHORUS 1

_____
_____

_____-

CHORUS 1

FADE

"ONCE UPON A TIME IN AMERICA"

9. Either   Male   Med.

Once upon a time in America. There was a little girl named Jessica. Her skin was dark, her hair was long but somebody told her she didn't belong. She spent all her life trying to be free, But the people wouldn't let her, just let her be. At age 25 she made the news, the headlines told how bad she'd been used.

CHORUS 1
Hurt, heartache, hopeless pain, There ain't no difference they're all the same. What we only hope is that there might be love. But that only happens once upon a time in America.

Little Bobby Stewart one day found a bag; It contained all the things you shouldn't have.
There was cash, needles, drugs and things, He didn't know the terror those things can bring.
He gave it to his mother so she could see. She said, "Bobby let's sell them so we can be free"…

(CHORUS 1)
Once upon a time in America, we only hope we get help from above.

REFRAIN 1
This is not a perfect world so many problems all around.
But we only hope we have the strength to love and let our love come out.…

(2) REFRAIN 1

CHORUS 1

(3) Dotta dotta da da da
(4) Once upon a time in America.

FADE

"I LOVE MY BROTHER"

10. Male

Pictures can never bring back the words yet I know you hear the heart.
Pain can never be fair in this world but my friend I wish we never had to part.

CHORUS 1
I weep for my brother and remember the times that we shared.
I love all my brothers and I care for all you out there…

Life is very fleeting you never know when it will take it's dare.
Give today every chance that you can and push the top of no matter where….

CHORUS 2
I weep for my brothers that have no proper place to go.
I love all my brothers and I don't mind letting
you know.

We love all the people of the world. They are our family.
Hug your mother, hug your father let them feel your love. And lady save a hug for me…

_____

_____

_____

CHORUS 1

FADE

"TRANSFORMATION"

11. Male Group   Pop   Med.

I couldn't believe that it was really you.
You looked like a whole new person brand new.
I never really took notice of you before But your sparkle hit me when you hit the door.

I can't believe the way your look has changed.
I thought for sure you'd always stay the same.
I never knew you but I wish I did.
I hope you don't remember the things I said.

CHORUS 1
You've gone thru a transformation.
There was never really any indication.
Now, you've got my full attention.
Girl, there's just one more thing to mention, You look good....

Girl it was a long, long time ago. I never thought I would see you no more. Don't you believe in forgive and forget. She smiled at me and said not a chance.

CHORUS 2
See she went thru a transformation, there was never any indication. She's got my full attention but she wants me to practice abstention.

I say (3) de da de de to de de ta de ta de
(2) da ta da to da da ta da ta da.

CHORUS 2

FADE

"YOUR A BETTER THING TO DO"

12. Male

There's a basketball game tonight but I won't be there,
A concert tomorrow but I won't show. You girl are all I need in my life and
with you I am never bored. Outside entertainment never do I want 'cause
to be with you excites my life enough.

CHORUS 1
(See) you fulfill me and give me what I need to survive
Nothing else really matters except my love for you, I'll give everything
baby because you're a better thing to do.

See my friends' they just don't understand. They say I'm henpecked and
I'm not being a man. I think they're jealous of the love share with you. I
don't care baby cause you're a better thing to do.

There's nothing in this world that I could ever think of, that would make
me give, give my love for you up.
They could offer me money and power and I would laugh in their face
'cause this love we have just can't be replaced…. NO,no.

CHORUS 1
(Cause)
For all my friends and things let my message read thru, it doesn't matter
what you want of me. My love is a better thing to do. She's a better thing
to do, now now. A better thing, a better thing, she's so good to me, She's a
better thing to do (3)

FADE

"I CAN'T GIVE YOU NO COMPLIMENTS"

13. Male
   Either
   Med.

Something in the way you carry yourself worries me, before I say something bad I think I'll go.

CHORUS 1
I can't give you no compliments
your not the one I'll give expense
Girl I think I'd rather climb a fence. If I brought you home mom would take offense.....

It's not that you're an ugly girl. Your problems not in the way you look.
See you must have one of the worst hearts in the world.
Baby your a dog in my book. How can I like you when all you do is lie.
You think the world centers around you. Friends are people who are honest to themselves. I guess I have to be honest with you.

CHORUS 1

_____

CHORUS 1

FADE

"TOMORROW IS A NEW DAY"

14. Male
    Pop.
    Med.

It's funny sometimes the way our memory works, we remember some things all our life and others we forget as soon as they end. But what really matters is that we can't change the past but we have all our to morrows to win....

REFRAIN 1
Forget about your frailties they don't have to last, nothing is forever.....
Take life by one day if you can and hope for the best....

CHORUS 1
So cry your tears now, let your emotion spring forth. Know that tomorrow might have something different to say 'cause tomorrow is a new day.

You put too much emphasis on one thing you did, Don't take life that way...Life is made of a collection of deeds that you do and remember tomorrow is a new day.

REFRAIN 1
CHORUS 1

REFRAIN 2
As long as you are kicking in this world, you have a chance to succeed. You can never give up on your life- —before —-has had it's last chance to breath...

So cry your tears now and let that emotion flow forth. Gather yourself, let me feel that strength cause girl tomorrow is a new day…

CHORUS 1
(2) Tomorrow is a new day,
Ad lib

FADE

"UGLY ATTITUDE"

15. Male
   RB
   UP

Just because you've been told that you're fine and beautiful,
 you seem to think that this should
give you the right to act a fool.
But let me tell you that to me you don't look that good,
always, cussing, always fussing and trying to do whatever you want to,
only tends to bring out your real ugly attitude.

CHORUS 1
Your ugly attitude comes from you
Makes you ugly even if you're nude.
Your ugly attitude is what shows
that's a shame too 'cause your body makes a man want to stand on his
toes.
Your ugly attitude comes from you
makes you ugly even if your nude.
Your ugly attitude is what shows you came in the front but you'll go out
the back door.

Only thinking about yourself is your problem.
You think it doesn't matter how you do it as long as you win.
With a better attitude there's no limit to what you could do. But instead
you're selfish and vulgar and that's the best they could say bout chu.

CHORUS 1

(4)Ugly, ugly, ugly attitude
CHORUS 1

FADE

"DETOUR"

16. Female
    RB
    UP

Every time I'm close to you, my heart smells your scent. Even if I try to turn away, my mind will try to build a fence.
I know I shouldn't be with you but I just can't help myself.
You're an experience I've never had before and I'm not ready to give up yet....

CHORUS 1
I take a detour to your heart baby. It doesn't matter where I'm going, cause with you I always end up.
I take a detour to your heart baby; you know of your love I can never get enough.
I take a detour to your heart baby; I don't know what's your hold on me but I hope you never lose your pump.

Verse 2
There's no replacement for the way you make me feel. Even though we know sometimes our love hurts to kill.
If I can have only part of your love then that's the way that it must be.
Cause the strength to give up your love is just not inside of me....

CHORUS 1
_____
_____
_____

Verse 2

CHORUS 1
I can never give you up, I just can't give you up.
Ad lib cont.

Fade

"YOU DON'T HAVE TO KNOCK"

17. Female
pop/ R.B.

It doesn't matter what I'm doing I'll make time for you.
I'll meet you anytime, anyplace.
You've got the features that I dream about.
You know I want you boy come fulfill my dreams.

CHORUS1
You don't have to knock to enter my world. For you my door is always open come make my heart twirl.
It will take all your love to satisfy me 'cause I will make sure you come back to please.

I'll give my body, my mind and my soul. I'll give you everything that you want. you know you're special that's what I see...
Let's not hesitate 'cause when together it will be ecstasy.

CHORUS 1
(3) You don't have to knock to enter my world.

(2) CHORUS 1

FADE

"WE'RE NOT MARRIED"

18.Female
   R.B.
   Med.

Baby I don't mind you giving me suggestions; I try to take what you tell me to heart. But when you persist on with your insistence. I think you take your role a little too far.

CHORUS 1
Baby remember we are not married, you have your place and I have mine. Your possessive attitude does not thrill me; I thought you'd learn that in time.

I can see this is gonna take some explaining. You understand only one way and kind. But baby relationships succeed with two commitments not when you say that's just fine.

CHORUS 2
See baby we are not married, you have your place and I have mine.
If you can't accept a different commitment, Then baby this could be our breaking time.
See baby we are not even married and you want me to do all you think is wrong or right. Well honey even if we are married you better believe we would have our fights.

REFRAIN 1
'Cause I'll never be someone's puppet, I love myself too much to be pulled. I could never be your fool 'cause then baby you'd be a fool too…

CHORUS 1
I'm not asking you to change, just open your eyes. Come on baby compromise.

REFRAIN 1
Won't you let love inside, let love inside, Won't you let it inside.

FADE

"YOU'RE WORTH THE PAIN"

19. Male
    RB
    Slow

When my friend said you are too much trouble I know what he meant because girl you want everything.
I work hard extra double and it seems like my energies all I spend...

CHORUS 1
(But) when you smile at me you rejuvenate my mind and when we make love it is one of a kind.
That special feeling is unique that you bring. Whatever the trouble you are worth the pain.

I know I could have someone who would cater to my will. But I know to baby that they wouldn't fit the bill. Tribulations and trouble I will take it all because to be with you is like a money windfall.

CHORUS 1
(Cause)...

REFRAIN 1
Girl you are worth the pain. The pleasure you give me makes my heart sustain.
Sometimes I think that it's time to give you up, but then I think about your love and yes I soon wake up.

CHORUS 1
(Cause)
REFRAIN 1

REFRAIN 2
Girl you're worth the pain, it hurts so bad makes me go insane. If you left me girl my life could never be the same, that's why whatever the trouble you are worth the pain.

CHORUS1
(Cause)…
Ad lib

FADE

"ARE YOU BETTER FRIENDS WITH THEM"

20. Male/group
    Pop/ Med

We grew up together, I thought we'd be friends forever. But all of a sudden things seemed to change, You and I were friends estranged....

REFRAIN 1
You let your fame take away our close but I don't know do you like that most.

CHORUS 1
Are you better friends with them? Do they know you better than I do? Will they be there till the end? Tell me, What's really special to you…to you, please tell me.

Once upon a time when our experiences were blind.
We said our friendship would always be true. But as life's nature took its toll those promises began to seem so old.
And all it seemed we wanted was experiences so new…

CHORUS 2
So tell me are you really better friends with them? Do they know you better than I do? Will they be there till the end? I don't know but please tell me what's important to you…to you, yeah.

REFRAIN 1
REFRAIN 2
Cause I'll be there till the end, You know I'll be your friend, with me you know you will always win.

CHORUS 2
REFRAIN 3
Do you know who is your friend? Will it ever be the same again? With me you know you can only win.

CHORUS 2
REFRAIN 2

FADE

"The Faith Of Love"

21.

Power comes in many different shapes and forms. Its measure can not be made on a scale cause if the power of love's faith had a form, it would reach to heaven evermore…

Refrain 1
Love's faith can keep you warm and joyful when it's cold and hard outside, It will be your shoulder to climb on when you need a ride. Love's faith can never ever be bought, faked or sold, The power of love's faith will always be untold…

CHORUS 1
There is no greater power than the faith of love.
It's a power given by that power high above.
You don't have to worry when you have the faith of love.
It will drive you, it will push to what you never dreamed of…

Love's faith is in your heart and soul. You can store it's power for a rainy .. day. With love's faith as your friend you will never be left cold. Love's faith will show the way….

REFRAIN 1
CHORUS 1
Love's faith is the spirit of your heart; It's power will never end. To be in love opens up your heart; It will give you the strength to win…

CHORUS 1
CHORUS 1
4 (It will show the way)

FADE

"YOUR LOVE IS ALL I WANT TONIGHT"

22. Male
   R.B.
   Slow Med.

There is nothing else that really matters tonight, tomorrow is so far away. You and I should be loving so tight. Girl this could be our fantasy...

CHORUS 1
Your love is all I want tonight, to give you ecstasy.
Hold your worries and your problems, let them drop out of sight.
Baby think only of me....

I don't care about tomorrow I want your love today, that's your effect on me. No, no I'm not sorry cause your love is all I need.

CHORUS 2
Your love is all I want tonight, to give me ecstasy. Girl You know this feels so right, baby share your love with me...

No more problems or excuses just love out of sight, baby you know the deal. Any reasons not to would be contrite, baby my love is real....

CHORUS 3
Your love is all I want tonight, can't help the way I feel. Girl all that matters is whether I am good tonight and tomorrow, whether our memories are filled.

I want your love tonight. Hey girl I want your love tonight. Hey girl I need your love tonight. This girl would be so very right. Just let me hold you tight....

CHORUS 2

FADE

"IT Doesn't Matter HOW LONG YOU TAKE"

23. Male
    Either
    Med.

Chorus 1
It doesn't matter how long you take, I'll still love you.
It could be forever and a day. I'll be here I promise you.

You can take a long trip baby, I'll keep your picture by my side. Never can distance lady make my love untie.
Love has lasted from long ago, Before biblical love time.
There is no way, shape or form for our love ever to decline.

CHORUS 1
Though we will be far apart our souls will be forever intertwined.
Our love is so very strong baby, it will stand all test from time.
Deep thoughts of you will fill my mind while we are apart. Love enemies will never win cause they'll never get a chance to start...

CHORUS 1
_____

_____

CHORUS 1
It doesn't matter how long you take, I'll still love you.
I'll be, I'll be, I'll be still in love. Still so much in love, so much in love baby.

CHORUS 1

FADE

"BETTER THINK ABOUT SOMETHING ELSE"

24. MALE
   R.B.
   Med.

If you've got that thought in your mind that I am a possession of yours, then you must be drinking that wine and baby you'd better find a cure. Cause if our love is ever going to be, then there is something that you have to see. Forever girl I will never wait for you to get what you want straight. I know I said I'd always be there for you but girl that's according to what you do. Cause if you think that you can string me long then girl I got news for you....

CHORUS 1
You'd better think about something else,
about being real and true with yourself.
See it seems our love is slipping, tell me girl what does it mean....

Girl what I really want is love. Something special and good to fill. If you can't figure what your made of, then girl I'll find someone who will... Tell me girl are you ready to love, ready to love, ready to love. Girl I know I am.

REFRAIN 1
Because I know there is love awaiting and I'll be ready to give it my all.
Girl you'd better be prepared to love me or be prepared to fall.

CHORUS1
If you want me to love you girl then you gotta love me. You can't have it both ways that's not the way this is gonna be...

REFRAIN 1

CHORUS 1
CHORUS1

FADE

"ARE YOU A PSYCHO"

25. Female
    R.B.
    UP

CHORUS 1
(Are you a psycho), very maniaco. If you can't take it tell me so, get up and hit the door.
Are you psychological, has anyone ever told you you need to grow. If not let me be the first to tell you so.

Just because I tell you no, you tell your friends I'm good to go. Have you ever been called medical, if not you must be frozen cold, girl you'll never see me in your hold.

CHORUS1
(You must be a psycho)..........................

Boy let me tell you your very po. I almost feel sorry for what you don't know. What's funny is you even asked for more, when you know good and well there was no before. Your problem is your ego and you better get it undertoe.

REFRAIN 1
Boy you better stop your lying, it will get you into trouble. Cause a girl's reputation is all of her honor...

CHORUS 1

_____

_____

CHORUS 1

FADE

"YOU MIGHT BE RIGHT"

28. Male   Pop   Med

You seem to know my state of mind at least that's the way it appears. My thoughts become so intertwined baby whenever you are near. See I think you cast a spell on me, even though I didn't see your wand. Girl your face is all that I see, what's happened to me?

CHORUS 1
If you think maybe I'm falling in love, you know you might be right.
If you say our friendship has become much more, you know you might be right.

I guess it snuck up on me. I didn't start out to fall in love; It wasn't a planned out thing. But girl my love for you came shining through and baby there can't be a better way.

CHORUS 1
If you think that I'm falling in love you know you might be right. Yea! If you say our friendship has become much more, you know you might be right.

Girl if you say it's right for you, you know it's right for me. Girl, You know its right.

Never did I think this situation would arise but I love this feeling when I look in your eyes. And you know what's funny girl, we may never have reached this part if we had never had a chance to start...

CHORUS 3
If you say this is the way love should feel, you know you might be right.

If you say this is the way love should feel girl, you know you're probably right. You know you're probably right…
CHORUS 1
(*) You know you're probably right.

FADE

"Hey Lady of A Thousand Suitors"

29. Male   Pop or RB   Slow-Med

REFRAIN 1
Hey lady of a thousand suitors which one suits you just fine.
Hey lady of a thousand suitors tell me what are you hoping to find.

If you are looking for diamonds you'll have no problem. They buy them to match your gorgeous face. If you want a man with fortune and fame. He will meet you anytime, anyplace.

CHORUS 1
(But) girl if you want love so deep, then girl you want me..
And girl if you want a forever love, then girl you want me…
Girl you want me, you want me.

REFRAIN 2
Because girl my love is real and everlasting and it's right here and now just for the asking. (Hey lady if you want love, want love, you want me.)

Hey lady of a thousand suitors what's really important in your life. Do you want a real commitment or do you want to play a gaming price.

REFRAIN 3
Hey girl if you're looking for understanding, you don't have to look very far baby. And if you're looking for love to last, girl no one could tear us apart…
REFRAIN 4
(2) Girl with my love there is a power, like nothing you've ever seen before. There's no reason to look any further because what I have is worth so much more…Much, much more baby.

REFRAIN 1
REFRAIN 3
They couldn't tear us apart.
REFRAIN 4
(Because)
Girl don't you want more, don't you want more.

REFRAIN 1
Girl if you really want love there will be no better time. (*) Won't you let love inside.

FADE

"I'VE BEEN THERE BEFORE"

30. Male   RB   Up Tempo/Med

I'm not fragile baby I'm a big boy now. If you're worried about hurting my feelings let your worries out.

REFRAIN 1
Cause I've been through the pain and I'm sure I'll see some more.
But I won't stop loving baby till there's love no more.
So realize baby I can handle anything you give.
You learn a few things if you live as long as I live.

CHORUS 1
So think about this when you enter out your door.
I can handle anything you give because I've been there before.

Don't worry bout me can you handle yourself; see I know what I'm doing like no one else. So be prepared when you enter my world. I t won't be long before I make your heart twirl. If you think you can handle it come on in because there won't be no denying when this good love begins.

CHORUS 1
REFRAIN

You must ask yourself a question now that you see. Do you think that you are ready can you handle me.

_____

_____

I can handle anything you give cause I've been there before. (4) Can you handle me.

FADE

"PAYDAY"

31. Male   Novelty/Country   Med.

Naw, darling I'm sorry I can't take you out. I can't tell you the reason but please don't shout.
Let's go out next Friday or Saturday see those are better days. She said, I know your reason and you really better find a way. See you went out with your friends and now you're broke. You better find some money quick or it's out the door.

CHORUS 1
Could you loan me some money till payday.
I will be in your debt for the rest of my days.
Just could you loan me some money for a little while.
I'll give back the money with my payday pile.

Sometimes at work I have nothing to chew. I tell them I'm on a diet but they know that's not true. See I don't always have enough money to please my girl but to please her I'd have to have all the money in the world.

CHORUS 1
My friends kinda frown when I come their way. They don't even wait to hear what I'm gonna say. They say hey where is that money from when I saw you last? I say I know owe money but I still must ask.

CHORUS 1
CHORUS 1

FADE

"BABY JESSICA"

32. Male   Either   Slow med.

Little lovely power touch the universe
She had a strong desire (for life) though life tried to give her a curse.
Wonder if we could be that strong in a watery darkened home.
For so very long (so very long) she was all alone....

CHORUS 1
Baby Jessica
The World loves you
Baby Jessica
So much pain came on you
Baby Jessica
But you found the strength

REFRAIN 1
You gave us hope, like we've seen never before, you didn't give up, you held the rope.
(Oh Baby Jessica)

Full of so much love you spread it across the seas.
Like a little baby dove, a shining pretty star of what we should be
Maybe you'll wear your scars forever, maybe they'll be in your dreams.
But in your times of trouble you always believe.

CHORUS 2
Baby Jessica
The World loves you.
Baby Jessica
Get your strength above you.

Baby Jessica
You gave us hope.

REFRAIN 2
With a heart of gold, you shed the fear, no turning back now, we'll always be here…
(Oh Baby Jessica)

CHORUS 1
CHORUS (Ad Lib)
REFRAIN 2

FADE

"JUST TOO HOT"

33. Male group   RB   Up Tempo

There's a fever going on and it's rising high.
We're going too raise the atmosphere out of sight .
Try to join in if you can keep up.
Cause to jam a little bit is just not enough.
We know what you need and were here to please.
You couldn't cool us down with extra freeze.
Gonna burn you up ready or not and there's nothing you can do because we're just too hot. Yea!
CHORUS 1
Get your head wet, make your body sweat.
Get down all night, till you drop from fright.
Get your attitude, set you in the mood.
Get your heart right cause will be up all night.
CHORUS 2
Ah do it real good, like you know you should.
Throw your cares away time to get down and play.
Don't let yourself stop, just go on and be too hot.

Can't stop us now were on the go. Before it gets too rough we'll try to let you know.
Don't mean nothing not trying to mess with you.
But you better call your mother don't know when we'll be thru.
Don't challenge us, we always win. You better find your finish cause we'll never end.
So get with the groove in this percolating pot. We're about to boil over cause we're just too hot. Yea!

CHORUS 2
CHORUS 1

CHORUS 3
Get your second wind party just begin.
Do your strong step till there's nothing left.
Do it real mean, go to all extremes.
Climb the mountain top cause you're just too hot.

Don't you know the deal it's time to be real.
Just let yourself go don't care who knows.
Twinkle, twinkle shining star we know you are.
The world's about to pop everything's getting just too hot.
Just too hot yea, just too hot.

CHORUS 1
(3) Can you keep up.

FADE

"SHENEE OF MY HEART"

34.
Your attraction took me by surprise.
I've never felt this way before.
But it was magic when I looked into your eyes.
Almost nothing could move me more.

REFRAIN 1
The thought of your love is the dream that I live for.
The thought of your love gives me power like never before.

REFRAIN 2
It gives me fire, gives me hope, gives me passion and lets it grow.
Your love is all that I need, girl I hope you honestly believe.

CHORUS 1
Your Shenee of my heart, girl I really want to love you.
Your Shenee of my heart, girl my thoughts are always of you.

You said I'm surprised when I told you my true feelings.
You said you say that to all the girls.
But I am hypnotized, girl please believe me.
For me there is no one else in the world.

REFRAIN 1

REFRAIN 3
You give me courage, give me strength. Girl my eyes just make me sink.
Your love is all that I need, please just honestly believe.

CHORUS 1
I tried to hold back my heart but your attraction was too strong. I tried to play the playing game but you made me play all wrong.
I hope one day, that you can share a part, of what I', feeling so strong deep inside my heart.
CHORUS 1
(4) La, la,la,la,lala, ala, la,la la

FADE

"BRAG ABOUT YOURSELF"

35. Male group   Pop/RB   UP

I used to be very modest, see never would I talk about me.
I finally came to realize that bragging is what you must do. Cause if you don't tell nobody how is someone gonna know about you.

See you must
CHORUS 1
(5) Brag about yourself (Do you believe in the concept of the deep.)

Now that I know what's happening never do I get low.
Cause if there comes up any question I never hesitate to show.
So if you find yourself a little stagnant cause someone doesn't believe in you.
Then you know your course of action and you know what you must do.

You've got to
CHORUS 1 (5)
(4) Brag about yourself
CHORUS 1 (5)

FADE

"WITH YOU CHRISTMAS IS REAL"

36. Male   Christmas   Med. Slow

At Christmas time everybody tries to put on a smile.
They say everything is beautiful and filled with cheer.
I usually see thru it all inside and out, But with you Christmas is real.
In the past I have never been very much on Christmas feelings.
But now I look at you and it starts me to believing. You are filled with every good emotion befitting this ultide occasion. Whenever I'm near you I'm filled with a new Christmas sensation.

CHORUS 1
With you Christmas is real, in your heart Santa Claus comes over the hill.
Your smile makes everyone feel joyous and gay.
Because of you for me Christmas is more than just a day.

Now I'm not saying that I'll believe in Christmas every year,
But everyday you're around Christmas is always here.
All those years I let my heart be cold and wouldn't let it listen.
But if this is the feeling I could have had oh my what have I been missing.

CHORUS !
Although the time is filled with false care.
People should beware cause your presence is in the air.
If someone ask me now, tell me Christmas what does it mean.
I'll say it means a time of hope-n-family and of your heart I'll always dream.

CHORUS 1

FADE

"I THINK I'LL MOVE AGAIN"

37. male   Pop   Med. Slow

I've moved a million miles from you but I still haven't gone anywhere at all. Cause wherever I move you still make my heart beat like a bouncing ball. Your scent smells up my every living room. Your face appears in all my mirrors, will my mind ever cease this gloom.

CHORUS 1
When am I gonna find my way.
When am I gonna find my place to stay.
Can I ever, will I ever get you off my mind.
I don't know, but I know I will continue to try.

Once I was your lover hugger but my how things can change so fast.
You just up and said to me one day that our love was in the past.
Sometimes ladies think that men don't feel any pain.
We might hold our hurt but it hurts just the same.

CHORUS 1
I don't want to move any more I think it's just a shame.
But for my peace of mind I think I'll have to move again.
Yes for my peace of mind, I think I'll move again.

FADE

"NOTHINGS HARDER THAN A ONE-SIDED LOVE AFFAIR"

38.

Sometimes love is blind, it just won't let you see. Can tend to make you lose your mind; but still I want to believe.
When you care for someone and they don't care for you. Can't get no help from nobody cause there's nothing you can do.

CHORUS 1
Nothings harder than a one-sided love affair,
When you want to love somebody and there's nobody loving there.
Nothings harder than being the only one in love, Cause the person that you love has other things they're thinking of.

So many times I've thought of giving it up. But I can't find the strength. Can't count the times I've said that's enough but girl now I'm pushed to the brink. Is there anything to do to end this pain, please put your knife through me girl don't let me go insane.

CHORUS 1

CHORUS 2
Nothings harder than loving the person of your dreams and that person doesn't tell you but she still lets you believe.
Nothings harder than really, really wanting to know but the person you love can't seem to find the strength to show.

(8) Don't string me long.

REFRAIN 1
Please just tell me, if you want me, please don't string me cause I love you. It's gonna hurt me, but please just crush me, If you don't want me, that's what you must do....

CHORUS 1
CHORUS 2

CHORUS 3
Nothings harder than loving someone in you're bones and when night comes you're always loving alone.
Nothings harder than loving with all your heart but you've been waiting forever for the other person's love to start.

(4) Nothings harder

CHORUS 1 Ad lib

FADE

"SHOW U OFF"

39. Male group   RB   Up Tempo

You look so good and so exciting, all of the men will envy me.
Matter of fact I'd like to tell you, that this feeling you give me just sets me free. To be with you many men would, try to be anything that you want them to be, but you girl are super special and that's what I want the whole wide world to see.

CHORUS 1
Got to show U off, to show U off,
I want the whole world to see.
Got to show U off, to show U off,
There's nothing better in the world to me.

Never before have I felt this way.
It's so good you should feel this way too.
Does wonders for your ego, makes your pride stand high.
Get those ripples through your body when you hear the people say oh my, my, my.

CHORUS 1
I can't believe that she is with me, must pinch myself everyday. When I hold her in my arms it assures me no doubt I will always find my way.

CHORUS 1

Ad Lib

CHORUS 1

FADE

"IF YOU'LL JUST HOLD MY HAND'"

40. Male Group   RB   Med. Slow

CHORUS 1
If you'll just hold my hand we could live forever. If you'll just hold my hand we'll fight the world together.

With you I am free, nothing is out of reach. I am at a loss without you, just your presence inspires me.
There's nothing we can't accomplish baby, no mountain too high.
Just give me your love lady and together, we'll learn how to fly…

CHORUS 1

CHORUS 2
If you'll just hold my hand what's old will be new.
If you'll just hold my hand I'll let my love shine thru.

Girl, I know you say your problems are here but girl hold my hand and I'll make you forget you had problems there.
Just give me your hand baby and together we will find a way.
You can hold your sorrows, better yet just throw them away. Girl don't worry, my love will, conquer all.
Nothing will stand in our way, we will always stand tall.

CHORUS 1

REFRAIN 1
If you want fame and fortune (fortune and fame) no bank can hold our stash.
If you want to go so far (go far) we'll go as far as far can.
If you want physical traction (physical traction) we will look so good.

If you want romance so sweet (so sweet) nobody will spoil our mood.

If you'll just hold my hand (4)

CHORUS 1
CHORUS 2

FADE

"THE TEACHER"

41. Male   Rap   Up Tempo

Hey everybody who wants to learn and even those who find books to burn.
I'm someone you need to know. I'm the teacher of life and I'm gonna start the show.
All you people who think you know what's up, take it from me you haven't learned enough. You learn something new everyday so open your ears hear what I've got to say.

CHORUS 1
I'm the Teacher
The Teacher
I'm the Teacher
The Teacher

REFRAIN 1
He's the teacher of what you should know.
He knows where you're going cause he's been there before.
He's the teacher of life, he knows how to win. He came up hard but he'll win in the end.

_____

Things are tough today, everything's going astray. If we didn't know better we'd say we're in the middle of a play. People will try to tell you anything cause they want to put you in the middle of their scene.
But if you'll listen to me, soon you'll see, that things really ain't as hard as they seem to be.
Cause the games played now have been played before, you just gotta tell how to open that door.

CHORUS 1

You know I could teach bout rap, teach you bout soul, teach you in the heat how to end up cold.
But the greatest lesson to give is the lesson of life cause that's a lesson that'll teach you how to end up nice. It takes survival you know, you got to be good to go, in other words always be ready to show.
I know you've heard it before but I'm a tell ya again, you never give in till your last   breath end.

CHORUS 1
There's only one way for you to succeed. Never give up, always believe in your dreams.

FADE

"I'll BUY YOURS IF YOU'LL BUY MINE"

42 MALE   POP   MED.

I'll buy yours if you'll buy mine, that's just the way it is. Nothing is for free. I'll take yours if you'll take mine, we have to learn to put up or it's time to leave.

Everybody tries to find that easy path but there are no roads easy.
We all must learn to give in half, cause no body will let you ride free.
We all must learn to compromise, to get what we want. It's time that we all realize, we must work to get up.

CHORUS 1
This world is full of politics, we must learn to give and take. Everyone ask how big your money clip, before they even see your face. There are those trying to find a better way, but the struggle is with them.
I listen to what that old man say, if you can't beat em join em.
CHORUS 1

CHORUS 2
I'll do you if you'll do me, we all must do something. That's just the way it is.
I'll like yours if you'll like mine, we can't like any.

CHORUS 3
I'll make yours if you'll make mine, see you when you get there.
I'll hurt you if you hurt me, tell me does anyone care...

CHORUS 1

FADE

"WHAT'S THE PRICE I HAVE TO PAY"

43. Male group   RB   Up

Baby, I wish, you had chosen a different profession cause I can't wait to get my hands on your body possessions.
You make super strange thoughts come to my mind, girl you must have been chiseled to be that fine.

It ought to be a crime not to share with the world, the dictionary of fine will carry your picture girl.
I"m sure wish you were a material lover, caused I'd pay any price to get you over.

CHORUS 1
What's the price I have to pay?
For one night with you I'll do whatever you say.
Let me tap your reservoir of love.
Girl give me what I need so much.

You could spur my energy eternal cause what you have is like lecticity burning.
Your body's built like a roundhouse right, who ever is with you must be praying for the night.
Just to look at you makes me tense. Thoughts go thru my mind, oh yes they are immense.
Girl if I could have you in bed there wouldn't be no doubt. The sounds you hear at night will be me screaming loud.

CHORUS 1

CHORUS 2

What's the price I have to pay, for one night with you I'll do whatever you say. Girl if we got together it would be so tough. Don't know if we'll stop cause I'll never get enough.

CHORUS 1 Ad lib

CHORUS 1

FADE

"FOR NO REASON AT ALL"

44. Male   *Pop*   *Slow Med.*

Does every question really have an answer. I wish I knew.
Life can be so confusing but I thought I'd always had you.
Sometimes we don't know how to get from A to Z; we can get lost in the
letters in between. But girl I always thought you'd be there for me. Never
did I think you'd leave…

CHORUS 1
Tell me why does man climb the mountain?
 Why is the water turned blue? Why does our heart beat like a bouncing
ball?
And tell why did you hurt me girl for no reason at all?

Everything doesn't always fir into right and wrong; for anything we can
find a gray between. For that pot of gold we've searched so very long.
Although we're living we still say life what does it mean? I don't know,
maybe I didn't hold your trust, maybe you lost your confidence in me.
But girl still know that I am so much in love; tell me girl why'd you set me
free…

CHORUS 2
Tell me why does man climb the mountain (when he's oh so high).
Why is the water turned blue. Why when we have planes do we still try to
fly. And why girl am I lost without you. Tell me why, why is finding love
so hard and why like raindrops we fall. I wish I had the answers and knew
in my heart and then I'd know why'd you hurt me girl for no reason at all.

CHORUS 1

CHORUS 2

For no reason at all, (2) No reason, (3) For no reason at all.

FADE

"FRONTAGE ROAD"

45. Male   Country   Med.

I am traveling well across the nation and I don't even have a map.
Don't like asking directions and I don't like taking a nap.
Try not to have any worries but the worries have caught up with me.
Cause I'm lost in Tuscalosa and I'm waiting for eyes to see.

CHORUS 1
(2) Frontage Road…
If I find then I know where to go.
(2) Frontage Road…
The road next to the highway and the road that will let you know.

Going with no directions is a better way to be. You don't have lot's of papers and there's a lot of things to see.
Of course you gotta have plenty gas and a whole lots of time. And you've gotta have lots of patience cause else you'll lose your mind.

Don't know what I'd do if I wasn't on the road. Don't really have a woman and nothing really strong to show.
If my friends say what's he doing, what's he really trying to see. Tell them I'm near my mistress, Frontage road is where I'll be….

CHORUS 1
CHORUS 1

CHORUS 1

She's the mistress of the highway and to find her I know where to go.

FADE

"YOU MUST BE A WRESTLING FAN"

46. Male   Country   Med.

Let me tell you about a guy at work who believes everything I say.
If I tell him I going to the moon you know he'll ask what day.
It would be awfully funny if it wasn't so, so sad.
There was nothing I could tell em except you must be a wrestling fan.

CHORUS 1
(2) You must be a wrestling fan...
You believe what you see cause you haven't learned the plan.
(2) You must be a wrestling...
You couldn't see the handwriting if it was right on the back of your hand.

Everything in this world has some elements of fake. It's got to the point where most things that you see ain't the same as what you think.
For instance if you think I can sing without your guitar you must be sipping a drink, cause everything's an image you just gotta know which one's complete.

CHORUS 1
Now I'm not saying those who I talk about are not good about what they do. But let them be compensated, they should be guild members too.
I like to see them swing and fight, it's an exciting thing to see. In fact between me and you, it's true they made a fan of me.

CHORUS 2
(2) You must be a wrestling fan
You believe what I see cause I haven't learned the plan.
(2) You must be a wrestling fan.

You couldn't see the handwriting if it was right on the back of your hand.

(2) You must be a wrestling fan

FADE

"SHE DOESN'T BELIEVE"

47. Male   Pop   Slow Med

When I first met her I loved her. Her attraction held me, I could only think of her. I told her how I felt she said no. She thought I was lying I tried to let her know. There's no stronger feeling than that first attraction. If you could harness the feeling, could make anything happen.

REFRAIN 1
Does she care how I truly feel? She might not now but one day she will. Cause what I have is a whole lot of love. My heart she can't resist. I'll give her what she's always dreamed of...

CHORUS 1
She doesn't believe I love her. She doesn't believe my every thought is of her. She doesn't know how much I need her. But a man in love will find a way to please her.

I don't know how she truly feels. Inside she may be laughing cause with my heart she can do as she will.
Yes, I guess my nose is open. She makes my mind so blind sometimes I can see nothing.
It may take some time but I'll win in the end, cause love has no timetable, it's good when it begins.
Although she has others trying to love her tonight, they won't measure up cause I love her with all my life....

CHORUS 1

CHORUS 2
She doesn't believe my world revolves around her. She inspires me I'm so glad I found her. She doesn't believe I'm the man of her dreams. She doesn't know now but one day she's gonna believe.

REFRAIN 1
REFRAIN 2
Girl one day you're gonna believe cause I'll bring the world right to your knees. You are my princess, you are my queen. There's nothing in this world together we can't achieve...

CHORUS 1
CHORUS 2

(5) She doesn't believe I love her.

FADE

"CHECK IS IN THE MAIL"

48. RAP

Everybody seems to want money from me. They must think my money really grows on trees. I know what you're saying I shouldn't have got all that debt but I like to spend money, I haven't spent enough yet.

Take it from me I know what's two times three, If you don't have credit then you don't have money. Cause credit is what the world is all about, if you don't have credit you don't have clout.

But hey all you hard up creditors, leave me alone, get off my ass.

Don't care how you scream, don't care how you trash, if you just be patient gonna get your cash.

CHORUS 1
My check is in the mail, please just wish me well. If you don't like it ring a bell cause I'm waiting for the sale.

You know money and me, we got a lot to see.

Some say money will set you free. Don't know about that but one thing I know, nobody wants to be friends when you got no money to show.

I remember not to long ago when I always thought my pocket had a burning hole. Bank tellers, store clerks and even the girls, said you've gotta have big money just to enter my world. But now that I have money don't know what's best. Cause I like to spend but collectors give me no time to rest.

CHORUS 1
Sometimes I have a longing for the simple days, when the first word out your mouth was not, "has your bill been paid". Wouldn't be nice if everybody could spend without having to end up paying in the end. Then everyone could share in all the fame and glory and not have to think it'd end up a tragic story. But it's not that way now, oh but can't you tell, please don't bother me cause my check is in the mail.

CHORUS 1
Hey Mr. Furniture man, let me be. Phone company don't take my phone away from me. Hey light company don't put me in the dark, what cha mean water man there's water in the park. Hey Mr. Rent man can't you wait another day. Please Repo man don't tow my car away. Well at least I have plenty of credit under the sun. Hey bank what ch talking bout insufficient funds.

(2) CHORUS 1

FADE

"I SHOULD BE IN HOLLYWOOD"

49.

I was rapping in the mirror the other day, found something out, didn't know what to say. Look at me, You can see, I'm the best.
Cause I'm prettier and smarter than all the rest. They just got there, had a break before I did. But there ain't no question I could do what they did.
All my friends always said you should be a star.
But they couldn't dream, can't believe, I would go this far.

REFRAIN 1
(4) I should be in Hollywood.
CHORUS 1
I should be in Hollywood, cause I think I'm looking good.
Won't say I wish I could, cause I'm gonna be there like I should.

All those others getting money for doing this and they don't get, I don't think, any type of welfare risk. All those others getting rich following this chilly plan and they can't be, I don't think as smart as I am. Prince, Michael Jackson even Simple Minds don't have, I don't think, any type of super minds, they just got there, had a break before I did. Hammer and LL I think I'm gonna do what you did.

REFRAIN 1
CHORUS 1
All those ladies living there, must be kinda nice.
Partying every night, now that's the life.
But someone said, yes he did, you must work, Yes I will. be no problem, gonna stay alert. Cause I'm the one that's gonna do it right, and when I get there you will see one hell of a night. Cause they will have one big problem, teacher Lou is now there to squab them.

REFRAIN 1

Gonna pack a bag, get fitted for a mike. Gonna ask that Bonet girl out the first night. All you ladies who felt you could have had me back then I'm so sorry now you should have had me back when. I gonna rock and roll and live freely like the old. Plan to live good and earn fortunes untold. Teaching job, family yes I know I did good but if you want to find me now I'm gonna be in Hollywood.

CHORUS 1
(The Girls)
(The Pain)
(The Life)
(Hollywood)

CHORUS 2

I'm gonna be in Hollywood, cause I know I'm looking good.
Won't say I wish I could, cause I'm gonna be in Hollywood.

CHORUS 2

FADE

"LOVE IS NOTHING WITHOUT LOVE"

50. Either   **Pop**   **Slow Med.**

I heard someone ask what is love, it's something were all hoping to find. But some people do a crazy look for love, they let strange thoughts enter their mind. They think love is a material thing.

Like something you can buy in a store. They think with money and flesh love will bring and even some let their friends tell where to find love's door.

But love is nothing you can just choose what you want, cause what love is, is so much more…

CHORUS 1

Love is nothing without love, without it you're still empty inside.

Cause unless you have someone who cares with all their heart, life will someday soon wash you aside.

REFRAIN 1

Love is not how much money you have. It's not how the body is toned. Love's a feeling deep in your heart, that someone else's love means more than your own.

Love is such a powerful resource, beyond our simple scope and dream. Nothing else can move us with so much force, it can make a strong man weak at the knees. We tend to forget sometimes that we are just flesh and blood, made of sand. But what makes us different is what's inside. Love's a feeling imbedded deep in our soul…

CHORUS 1
REFRAIN 1

BENU AND EDUCATION

"Bennu" means the redemption and reconciliation of the soul, a spiritual rebirth. In Ancient Egyptian theology it is represented by a bird with long life .This ancient symbol represents the combination of spirit and intelligence necessary for holistic growth and advancement in society. 1. *Light From Ancient Africa, Naim Akbar 2. Nile Valley Civilizations, Anthony Browder*

Overall education in our society has fallen into a deep low well. It is in need of redemption. Not just education of our youth but education of all our people. Drugs and crime are decimating our society. There is a substance missing in our day to day lives. Society today is filled with high technology and many different kinds of gadgets to supposedly make life easier but ask most people today and they will tell you there is more pressure and more stress than ever before. There is a difference between the way children actually learn and they way we are trying to teach them.

Children and all human beings learn through their senses. Normally we are taught we have five senses. We have a sense of hearing, a sense of touch, a sense of taste, a sense of sight and a sense of smell. But these observable phenomena were only representations and symbols of the spiritual reality according to researchers. Some have found we have two other senses. We have a sense of intuition and a sense of divine connection.

Certain emotions create a system of vibrations from people that can actually be sensed without words. 1

This is the intuition capacity that we all have and can develop. From birth we are born with a divine connection and ethics of right and wrong that do not have to be given to us in a list. These gifts are imbedded in our conscienceness as human beings.

Children and all human beings have needs that need to be met to become Self Actualized or reach full development as human beings. Maslows calls these the "Hierarchy of Needs". He conceived of five levels of needs arranged in a sequence from lower needs to higher needs:

1. *Physiological needs* (for example, to satisfy hunger and thirst.)
2. *Safety needs* (for example, to maintain security, order, and stability.)
3. *Belongingness and love needs* (for example, to receive affection and identification.)
4. *Esteem needs* (for example, to experience prestige, success, and self
respect.)
5. *Self Actualization* needs.

3.*Maslow (1954) Mental Retardation, A Life Cycle Approach. Drew/ Logan/ Hardman 1984

Forty three years after the historic civil rights case of Brown versus the Board of Education, Public education is far from the color blind, multi-cultural school environment the dismantling of legal segregation was supposed to bring about. Public schools have become a maze of violence, apathy and uncertainty.

As larger society continues to erode, the public school continues to reflect the worst of our society because children don't know how to hide their emotions like we as adults supposedly do. Children are open, warts and all. They reflect the true culture of our society.

The dismantling of legal segregation brought great hope to those who felt that a color blind society was the best thing for everyone. Black people felt they were finally going to be allowed to participate in the American dream. Many diversity programs were begun. Across the country school busing began, Minority to majority programs were implemented and Multi cultural perspectives were encouraged.

The idea was to mesh those who had been left out of the melting pot (blacks) and other minorities with those who were on the inside(whites) . What would result they said was a utopic blend of humanity breaking down previously limited borders of understanding and accomplishment. A new frontier of cooperation would occur.

But as children are a true reflection of society, they correctly modeled our behavior. They reflect our fears, our jealousies and our envies. They reflect our greediness and our spite. The problems with public education in America are the weaknesses of our society. The problems are much bigger than our education system can deal with. There is an extreme deluge and gulf of lack of feeling our students are in today. The Columbine murders, the first grader who committed murder and many other child acts of violence are indicative of the horrible state of mind our children are in. But, how do we teach values in a spiraling destructive country.

The problem of education in today's society is a problem of psychology. Our children and people often times do not feel worthy. Many of us struggle with inferiority and this feeling passes through generations. Jaromogi Abebe Agyeman (Rev Albert Cleage), founder of The Shrine of The Black Madonna and a noted educator states*" The problem of Inner City Schools raises basic psychological problems for many black parents because they are not yet convinced of the intellectual equality of either themselves or their children"*. 4 The curriculum, the structure of the system (television, sports, entertainment, etc) and legal and social framework all work to perpetuate white cultural supremacy and ineffective educational growth especially for African American students. But what effects black students affects all students and becomes a problem for all of society. African American students are products of the most destructive types of negative conditioning. An example of this type of insanity can be seen in the firing of a 20 year teacher in New York City. Yaa Asantewa Nzinga was fired because she taught her class they were original Africans not Americans. Black people were taught to hate themselves and our still suffering from that teaching.

Jaromogi further adds, *"When you don't belong to anything, when you don't have any hope, you are in the process of degenerating into a monster. When you don't have any attachment, any identification, you ask yourself, "Who Am I", I don't belong to a people. The answer is clear and inescapable".* 4

His answer, Children and adults on the fringe will get by the best they can and take care of themselves the best they can.

The educational system in this country must go through drastic change. Educational vouchers is one change we can implement to bring about a better system.

The New Bush Administration is leaning toward faith based learning institutions being a greater standard in America. Parental school choice or vouchers are an important part of this new policy.

Many people assume vouchers would only benefit the already rich and leave minorities and the poor without foundation. According to Gwen day Richardson, (Headway Magazine), "A majority of the grass rots organizations supporting vouchers and school choice programs are from black communities. 5 Blacks Take The Lead on School Choice, USA Today August 22, 1997

A recent survey by the Joint Center for Political Studies showed that 57% percent of blacks supported school vouchers for public, private or parochial schools-while whites split evenly and it further found that support for vouchers among African-Americans increased by 10% between 1996 and 1997. (1998)

Educational vouchers are not the only answers to improve schools. Schools need increased discipline, better pay for teachers and high expectations. However, one of the biggest factors in continued school apathy is the mind set the children have of getting something for nothing. School is too valuable to society to allow students to believe it is easy to come by. American voters of all races and parties voice general agreement on the importance of personal responsibility, that hard work pays off and that people shouldn't blame others for their failures, according to the Post/Kaiser/Harvard Survey.

Many teachers will tell you the problem is not a lack of money or dedicated teachers but an overwhelming apathy and lack of desire that students bring with them into the school. And that apathy transcends to a lack of respect for teachers, violent outburst and other maladjusted behaviors unacceptable to society. What history shows is that the problems of high spending, lack of successful innovation, unresponsiveness to the needs of families, and social strife over what is taught are mainly caused by the way public schools are run, not by the people who staff them or the particular standards or curricula they adopt. 6. Why We Should Consider Alternatives to Public Schooling", Andrew Colson, School Choices. Org 1998.

Educational vouchers would change the focus away from educating all students to educating students who have a desire to learn. Teachers should not have to spend the majority of their time with two or three bad apples who are disrupting the learning process. We should concentrate our efforts on those students who wish to learn and provide alternate schooling (Maybe the new role of Public education) for the other students who have problems.

Integration has provided access to better facilities and opportunity for black children. However, there is a difference between access and integration. All children deserve the best resources available for our tax dollar.

But that does not necessarily mean the best opportunity is sitting next to a student of another race. The greatest factor toward providing proper educational advancement is a stimulating environment. The best environment can be provided by teachers, administrators and a community that cares and understands the needs of the students in their classroom. Education and discipline are the keys to growth.

Black Educational achievement from kindergarten through high school has been rising for the past two decades. Evidence suggest that the credit lies with the increasing amount of education attained by black parents, not with desegregation or compensatory education. 7. With vouchers Black parents have a greater flexibility to find the best education available. Representative William Crawford, a Black Democrat in the Indiana legislature said. "A voucher program would empower parents to choose. There is nothing wrong with empowering parents to make choices". 7 Indiana's Moral Battle on School Vouchers, Washington Post .com Thomas B. Edsall, Oct. 19,1998

Our schools must have a system which is concerned with teaching community values to the children. The first place to learn values is in the home. The neighborhoods must and should be an extension of the home and everyone who is apart of the community must take some responsibility for the development of the children. All children have a right to know about those from their community who have done remarkable things. What inspires the child should be the most important thing and each community should have the right to choose the role model's important to them.

Every community should concentrate on their own history which would reflect the accomplishments of those whom are important to them while at the same time learn about and respect every groups history.

Real education is the key to understanding and the community is the base of love that must nurture the child.

Our society must make a drastic change in how it looks at education. A compulsatory public academic education system is not working and not serving its purpose of providing for a better overall education for all American students. At the age of thirteen or at the beginning of the eight grade students should be given the choice of staying on a path of academic training, structure their training for industrial or technical careers or let them go to work. No matter what steps we take we will never achieve 100 percent of all students learning. Every student can not be educated nor has a desire to be educated. But we can create the opportunity for every child to have a education if they so desire. And we must make education attractive.

What are educational system must provide is opportunity and make sure all children have a chance for the best education possible. Public Education should provide advance training in specialized schools with disciplines in engineering, medicine, computer science, industrial art, etc. It could be patterned similar to the magnet school system in Houston, Texas.

The magnet school channeled students who wanted to concentrate on certain disciplines and put them in a school with an emphasis on that discipline. For instance, students who wanted an Engineering career went to High School for the Engineering Professions. Those students who wanted to become doctors or nurses went to High School for the Health Professions. Students who wanted a career in Law Enforcement or Legal work went to The High School for Criminal Justice. If students were interested in Industrial Arts or Technology they went to Barbara Jordan High School . There was a school available for every interest a student might have.

These schools should have advanced standards and high expectations. However, all students will not achieve in this environment.

Alternative schooling which provides instruction at a less advanced paced should be provided for students who do not achieve at the high academic schools. But the emphasis of these school should be discipline and behavior modification. Students must be guided to have the proper behavior and discipline to achieve and special attention must be placed on their needs before they can achieve full academic potential. Meeting the needs of children with learning disabilities must also be a component of Alternative schools.

Very important to the success of children in all school environments is we not allow a negative stigma be attached to any of these schools. They must be made to feel wanted .

However, if children are not able to achieve in either environment, parents must have the option of sending their child to a private school if they believe they can get a better education there.

New teaching innovations should be tried such as *"Honors Integrated Competitive Learning"* 8 which teaches children how to effectively master two or more activities at the same time. Measurement of success must be holistic.Handwritten test are an important testing tool but equally important measurements should be peer group interaction, arts and craft interpretative measurement and oral basic skills test among others. No one measurement tool can give an accurate accounting of a child's ability. Many measurement tools must be given in combination to be accurate.

We agree with President Bush , No child should be trapped in an endless cycle of non progress and if a voucher, private school program can help we should do it. It is up to the community with government support to make sure no child is left behind . The emphasis on Faith Based institutions can help to foster greater cooperation in the communities.

Children must be inundated with the qualities of scholarship, discipline and responsibility. Further innovations could be to have residential schools where children 6 through 13 could stay at a school Monday-Friday full time and have a light television diet but a very heavy computer diet. Students would go home only on weekends to be with their families.

Discipline and safety should be strictly enforced. Metal detectors could guard against firearms or weapons on campus.

However, the most significant aspect of change could be to give our teachers proper payment for teaching and proper security with limited peace power to direct bailiffs or security aids to remove or detain students deemed disruptive, unruly or in contempt. Of course with a voucher program students who do not want to be in school would not be required to come and if they can't live up to the standards of the competing institution they could be dismissed and sent to alternative schooling. As Black people we should not be afraid of vouchers but should be open to them. We could then teach our curriculum in our faith based institutions with a special emphasis. We have a lot to unlearn.

We must undertake a mission of redemption and reconciliation of our whole process of education and nurturing our people. Vouchers would help take away a permissive and don't care attitude that permeates the public school system. Each school should have their own rules and standards which would govern their institutions. Government still has a responsibility to insure the intellectual future of our nation. They have a significant role to play. But that does not mean they have to provide the day to day operations of education, (Public schools).

But they can serve as watchdogs for the community much like the FCC watches the Radio and TV industry. They can provide educational grants or subsidies to make sure needy families have the same opportunity for a quality education that wealthy families have.

Education is too important to play with and should be treated as such. *"If we don't put it together, nobody else will and our children our going to be destroyed and if they are destroyed, we will be destroyed with them…perhaps by them.* Jaromogi pg 240

The Crisis of Public Schools is not necessarily a bad thing, it is according to how we handle it.

The system of education of the Ancients

holds a pathway to a new psychological framework of learning for our children and our society. In this framework are the pathways back to the proper order., which include the journey's of redemption: restoration, and resurrection, 1r.

It may be the catalyst we need to create the best educational system in the world.

by Baruti and The Honorable Raymond Alexander , Former Member of the State Board of Education for the State of Texas

Reflections: (The More I Learn.)

This excursion of life goes through many travels. As we continue to learn, we adjust, adapt and change from the beliefs we had yesterday. One thing I've learned is those who never admit they don't have all the answers are those who are starting with a lie.

In my journey I have come across many understandings and beliefs but the one constant is GOD. GOD's DIVINE ORDER remains the same. Whatever interpretation of GOD's destiny we have, there is no dispute that some eternal force leads and guides us.

Many of the writings I did in the first edition I look back upon today and laugh or maybe even cringe at but they truly reflect the feelings I had at the time I wrote them. The essays still reflect the essence of my beliefs. What is it that I believe today? Has anything changed in the last ten years?

I believe the more I learn the more I know. That is how I kind of see myself. We don't know what we can do until we try and everyday is a new opportunity to do better. We are at our best when we plan for tomorrow but recognize that destiny is not promised to us; we have to make it happen. And even the best plan can go astray and we have to find a way to pick ourselves up and go on.

The essay on "Bennu and Education shares some of my beliefs about the current educational system and the need for Spiritual Recovery in our society today.

I believe my mission is to first seek out and save that inside of me which is lost and then help others do the same. But that also is an ongoing progress which must be done at the same time. Many strong, talented and beautiful people are being lost to the demons of this world and we must fight against them so as to not allow them to consume our lives or others. We are created with the power. GOD willing, my eyes have been given sight and my feet have been led on the right path. There is no more important mission than the redemption of our souls. The trials of the fire are just beginning. I am blessed and thankful to have been given the opportunity to share my heart with you.

Sincerely; Carl L. Alexander
(BARUTI)

About the Author

"Though you may have been blind the sun still shines, The fire still burns like a slow ,powerful ember waiting to spark and come alive"

Born February 14, 1962, Baruti always wanted to be a writer. Growing up he was very shy and found the written word as a way of expressing his true self. Baruti earned a B. A. in Journalism in 1985 from Texas Southern University.

After a decade as a teacher, He decided to pursue his lifelong dream of being a writer and life teacher. He has been influenced by the teachings of Jaromogi Abebe Aygeman , Minister Farrakhan and many others. Baruti studies many theologies but his mission is the liberation of African and all people in need of spiritual recovery. He continues to seek divine connection with the supreme being that governs nature and the universe. Umoga, Ujamma, Uhuru!

Baruti Ambakiseye